Trust Your Step

How a Leap of Faith Led to an Amazing
Adventure

Alise M. Oliver

Edited by Nancy Pile: www.zoowrite.com
Cover Design by pro_ebookcovers
Cover Photo by Alise Oliver
Formatted by Debbie Lum: debbie@debbiestevenlum.com

www.alisesamazingadventure.com
ISBN-13: 978-0692062005

To My Favorite

Contents

Introduction

In the spring of 2014, I came across the following quote: "You are in the driver's seat of your own life."

I stared at the words for a long time, and suddenly it hit me how true that was. As I reflected on my life, I had always believed that I was a helpless passenger in the seat of life. That life was just randomly driving me around. Sometimes it would deliver me to a fantastic destination, but at other times I would be taken to someplace awful, entirely against my will. It was as if I had absolutely no say in where I was going. I would feel betrayed by life and think, "Why am I here? I'm trapped and I can't get out. And I have no choice."

I next realized that my riding-in-the-passenger's-seat mentality was entirely untrue. In fact, *I* was the one who was driving. *I* was choosing the route. Whenever I ended up somewhere I didn't want to be, it was entirely *my* doing.

Finally, I realized I was not a victim of life. Everything happened as a result of the choices I made; it was entirely my responsibility. If something in my life was not leading me to a state of peace, it was entirely up to me to change the course to put myself on the road to peace.

It was an incredible and powerful realization. I could choose the route. I could choose the direction I would like to go. It was the birth of my Amazing Adventure.

* * *

I decided to change the direction of my life. I gave away all my extraneous stuff. I put my house on the market, set a date to quit my job, put my personal belongings in storage, and planned a three-month road trip around the country. I wanted to visit friends whom I had not seen in years, visit places I'd always wanted to see, do CrossFit along the way, take some pictures, write a blog, journal, and see what life had in store for me.

After the trip I could return to Louisville, Kentucky, where I'd been living for the past 17 years, or I might find someplace else to call home. I was completely open to the Universe.

I kept looking at this quote over and over again: "And if life only teaches you one thing, let it be that taking a passionate leap is always worth it. Even if you have no idea where you're going to land, be brave enough to step up to the edge of the unknown, and listen to your heart." Yes, I was listening to my heart and stepping up to the edge of the unknown. The thought of the trip gave me an incredible feeling of peace. I'd never taken that kind of time for myself, and it was the perfect opportunity.

Over the course of those three months, I visited many old and new friends, some of whom I hadn't seen in over 20 years. I traveled 16,000 miles in my trusty Toyota Matrix through almost every single state in the country. I ate delicious food, drank new tasty beer, and dropped in at several CrossFit gyms to work it all off. I visited ten national parks and several other national landmarks. I saw such incredible beauty that many times I was in awe and moved to tears.

Most important of all, I learned about myself: my fears, limiting beliefs, and habits. I learned about letting go, letting go of my comfort zone and safety net. Letting go of needing the approval of others. Letting go of trying so hard to figure things out. Letting go of worry.

I also discovered wonderful things about myself that I'd never realized or acknowledged. I love to drive and drive long distances! I learned that I love to have the freedom for some solitude, but that I really don't like to be alone. I learned that I'm not really shy at all, and I actually enjoy talking to strangers. I discovered that I'm not unapproachable or intimidating; I'm open, friendly, and happy, and people really like to be around me. I learned that I can be flexible and spontaneous. I learned that I am strong, brave, and courageous, that I am enough, and that I am worthy.

Through my experiences I hope that you, my reader, recognize these beliefs and patterns, and discover that, like me, you can find a happier, more fulfilling life. It's simply a matter of listening to your heart and trusting your step.

Preface

If you want something you've never had, you have to do something you've never done.

It was a typical dreary winter day in Louisville, but inside the Irish Rover, the pint of Guinness I drank and the company I shared lifted my spirits. I sat across the worn wooden table from my friends, Brooks and Linda, holding on to every word Brooks said to me.

We'd met up at the Irish Rover for lunch, and I poured out my heart to them: my discontent with my job and my life, and my desire to make a change, but my fear blocking me from imagining what that could be.

With Guinness and Irish whiskey flowing freely, the ever-confident Brooks emphatically declared, "If you're unhappy with the way your life is going—it's like you're on a train, and you just gotta jolt that train *completely* off that old set of tracks onto a brand-new set!"

With these words I felt an excitement build inside me that anything was possible.

CHAPTER 1

The Catalyst

And if life only teaches you one thing, let it be that taking a passionate leap is always worth it. Even if you have no idea where you're going to land, be brave enough to step up to the edge of the unknown and listen to your heart.

It was a sunny but bitterly cold January morning. I was driving to work when my phone rang. I pulled my car over to take the call.

After the call ended, I sat there in stunned disbelief, heart pounding, sick to my stomach. Kat, my partner of five years, had just broken up with me.

I quickly turned the car around and drove to my sanctuary, Derby City CrossFit (DCCF), where my best friend Erin had just finished coaching the 8 a.m. class. Bursting into tears, I told her the news.

I spent the next few weeks in a daze of heartbreak, non-stop crying, and immense grief. Although deep in my soul I'd known that the relationship was not working, I didn't want to believe the breakup was really happening. I had tried so hard, over and over, with every setback, never wanting to give up on it.

Fortunately, I had an incredible support group available to me—my family, my friends at both DCCF and the YMCA, my two best friends Patti and Erin, and my friends in the community chorus of which I was serving as interim artistic director. My friends and family all seemed to have much more faith in me than I ever had in myself.

As I worked through the grief of the breakup, I started to look closely at every facet of my life with an honesty I'd never been able to apply before. I admitted to myself that I was terribly unhappy in most facets of my life.

The five-year relationship with Kat had been a tumultuous one. We had met in the fall of 2009 when she joined the community chorus in which I sang. She was kind and caring, had a wonderful laugh, deep blue eyes, and a gorgeous smile. We seemed to be on a similar path of New Age spirituality and self-development.

As the years passed though, the relationship sputtered and stalled. There was no doubt I loved her, but I had an avoidance pattern, which kept me from being able to fully commit to her. Whenever Kat would voice her desire for more emotional connection to me, I would withdraw, but then slowly re-engage with her. Each time this happened, we'd talk and talk about it, and I tried to do better with the tools that I had at that time to try to fix it or make it work. This roller coaster continued for years.

Finally, in May of the previous year, hoping to break my pattern and actually commit to the relationship, Kat and her three kids moved in with me. Although I made an effort, I was ill equipped to handle the change. It was extremely difficult for me to lose my feeling of control and adjust to four other people living with me. After five years of living by myself, I found it especially difficult to adjust to the normal kid stuff—the clutter, the noise, the occasional outbursts and arguments. As the months progressed, I withdrew more and more, and our relationship deteriorated.

The final straw was my complete inability to support her emotionally when her mother passed away. I kept my distance, taking care of the household, but I just didn't have the emotional intelligence to recognize that what she really needed was for me to be with her, at her mother's side in the hospital. Although we tried a last-ditch effort of couples counseling at the end of that year, I was defensive and unable to accept responsibility for my actions and behavior and how that affected her. There would be no turning back.

My job was no better. I had been working for Kentucky Opera for 15 years after two years as the assistant professor of horn at the University of Louisville. I was planning to work for the company only until I got another teaching position, but that never happened. With each passing year, my restlessness increased. I looked at my coworkers and my boss, most of whom had a passion for opera and their jobs. I enjoyed parts of my job, but it never truly inspired me. I felt trapped and angry as I stayed in a job that did not fulfill my own passion for teaching and inspiring others.

* * *

Several years earlier, I had joined a local gym and participated in several group fitness classes. About a year later, my favorite spin instructor arranged for some class members to visit a local CrossFit box (gym), Derby City CrossFit. At the time, CrossFit was fairly new, and the method of training via functional movements, which combined weightlifting, plyometrics, gymnastics, and high intensity interval training, was a new concept.

After the first visit to DCCF, I was hooked. It varied every day, it challenged me like nothing else had, and I felt part of a really close community. CrossFit became such an important aspect of my life that throughout the next several years, I became a level 1 certified instructor and began coaching at DCCF. I also attained my personal training certification and started coaching a group fitness class that I created at a branch of the local YMCA. It was at DCCF that I met Erin, and we quickly became inseparable 5 a.m. classmates.

After a few years, Erin and I started taking steps towards opening our own gym, and I'd gone as far as refinancing my house to get a small equity loan as part of my buy-in to the business. At the same time, Erin had slowly started her own garage gym and online nutritional counseling service.

As she settled into her dream, I felt like my dream was over, and I was too insecure and fearful to try to venture into a career change alone. I loved coaching and had a passion for it. I had a gift to be able to motivate and inspire people to do more than they thought they were capable of doing. It was incredibly gratifying to help my class members realize that they were stronger than they thought. I felt so unsure of myself though, that I didn't think I could support myself on coaching alone.

After my dream of finally being able to quit my day job and do something I loved slipped away, I was even more desperately unhappy at the opera. However, I convinced myself that I would never be able to get another job and I couldn't quit. It was a steady paycheck, offered health benefits, and paid the mortgage for my house, which I was determined to hold onto no matter what. I felt completely trapped.

* * *

The first weekend of February was difficult. My partner—make that my ex-partner—would be moving the remainder of her things out of the house. Fortunately, I was spending the weekend in Lexington, Kentucky, at a women's training seminar.

As I pulled into the parking structure of the Hilton in downtown Lexington, I took a glance at my Facebook page. I noticed that Patti had posted to it. I clicked on it and saw an image of a woman at the edge of a precipice, about to bungee jump off into the beyond. There was a quote by Iyanla Vanzant along with it:

> *Each of us faces a moment in our lives called the breakdown moment. This is the time when you must stand toe to toe, eyeball to eyeball, with the very thing you have tried desperately to avoid. In that moment, when there is nothing standing between you and the thing you fear the most, you will be forced to step into greatness, because that is what life is demanding of you.*

I broke down in tears. I was at that breakdown moment. I feared aloneness, I feared having to depend solely upon myself, I feared letting go of any and all security I had left in my life.

But I'd gotten to the point where staying in my unhappy life was scarier than the fear of change.

I was at a crossroads.

* * *

As the weeks passed, my thoughts started expanding outside the box for the first time ever. It dawned on me that if I didn't have my house payment, if I downsized to a small condo, perhaps I wouldn't need that job in which I was so unhappy. Maybe then I could make it by doing what made me happy.

At the same time, I was feeling a need to escape—I longed to visit my best friend in Greensboro, North Carolina, and old friends in Iowa. I thought over and over, "Wouldn't it be great if I could just get away for a few weeks and see my old friends? How could all that be possible?"

Suddenly Brooks' advice from over a year earlier came hurtling back to me like a thunderbolt: "If you're unhappy with the way your life is going—it's like you're on a train, and you just gotta jolt that train completely off that old set of tracks onto a brand-new set!"

It suddenly dawned on me: if I sold my house, not only would I not have that mortgage payment or need the job that I hated, but also I could get away like I wanted to. I would have the time to see my friends across the country.

My thoughts started snowballing: I could take longer than a few weeks. I could get in my car and take a road trip around the country, see ALL my friends all over the country. I could visit cities and states I'd never seen. I longed to visit the Atlantic, the Gulf, the Pacific, to sit on the beach, dip my toes in the water, and watch the sunrise and the sunset. I'd never been out West, and for some reason my soul was calling me there. I was fascinated with and drawn to Montana—I longed to experience the "immensity of the sky," which I was certain was there.

The more I let my mind wander, the more and more places I thought of. I imagined visiting CrossFit gyms around the country. I thought of the national parks I'd never visited and the pictures I could take. I imagined writing my own blog about all the self-discoveries I was making along the way. I imagined finding another city that might call me and possibly become a new home. I could finally find myself.

An excitement, which I'd never felt before, slowly began to fill my soul, and the more I thought about this trip, the more I was filled with an incredible peace. I looked around my little house—my safety net, my wonderful, cute, fabulous house with all its memories, good and bad—and for once I didn't feel a desperate need to hold onto it. It was a wonderful house, but I slowly realized it had served its purpose.

I emailed my realtor and good friend, Bob German, asking, "What would it take to sell my house?"

I bought a map of the United States that was the size of my dining room table and circled the cities where all my friends lived. I circled cities where my family members lived. I circled all the cities I've always wanted to visit or been told were wonderful to visit. I circled all the national parks I could think of—Grand Canyon, Glacier, Yellowstone, Yosemite. I looked at my map, and all my circles connected into one huge, smooth, round path around the United States. It looked so right, and it felt so perfect.

The following weekend, my best friends and I went out to dinner. Waiting for a lull in the conversation, I gathered my courage, took a deep breath, and shared my plan. It was scary; so many thoughts had been racing through my mind. Would they think I was foolish, crazy, impulsive, unwise to sell my house, quit my job, and just take off? But my fears were unfounded. Without exception, they were overwhelmingly supportive, positive, and happy for my courage to take a leap of faith.

Inspired by that victory, I emailed my dear friend Tonya the next day. Three years previously, she'd done the exact thing I was contemplating—quit her job, sold her stuff, drove cross-country, and found herself in Sedona, Arizona, where she has been ever since. I knew that she would relate to what was going on in my life and my reasons behind the desire to leave everything behind and find my true self.

I was overwhelmed with emotion when she immediately fired back a two-page email completely supporting my decision (in fact, she wrote, "LEAVE RIGHT NOW") and inviting me to visit her in Sedona.

Riding the wave of approval, I emailed all my siblings the next day. I was nervous to share the news. I was especially anxious about my oldest brother's reaction. He's very traditional and conservative, and I was concerned that he might think it imprudent of me to give up the security of my job. I was overcome with emotion when I heard back from him immediately, before anyone else:

As conservative as I am, I think this is a good move for you. Our discussion a couple of weeks ago made it apparent to me you were at a crossroads. Going to the next step of reevaluating your life, where you are at and where you are going, is a natural. Good for you to be able to take this step and create for yourself the circumstance that allows you to step back and look forward to the future while experiencing new things that the travel will avail to you. Perhaps re-reading

Travels with Charley by John Steinbeck will be a good primer for the forthcoming events.

Relief washed over me. The rest of my siblings and siblings-in-law responded just as enthusiastically and positively.

Finally, I made the hardest call of all, the one to my mom. Although I knew she was keenly aware of my unhappiness, I was worried that she wouldn't approve of my idea. My worries were quickly dispelled as she rejoiced at my courage and was excited at the description of my proposed path.

The journey was on!

CHAPTER 2
A New Chapter

If you're brave enough to say goodbye, life will reward you with a new hello.

The day finally arrived. I said farewell to the friends who had become my family and the city that had become my home for the last 17 years.

I remembered when I first moved to Louisville. That was August 22, 1997. It had not been an easy adjustment for me. My hometown of Naperville was only five hours north, but there was a different culture "down south" in Louisville than I was used to. People seemed to move and speak a bit too slowly, the southern twang took some getting used to, and I almost felt like a pushy impatient Yankee compared to all the Louisville natives.

I remember driving to my job at the School of Music at U of L in the mornings and thinking, "I hate it here . . . It's so daunting, I don't know anyone, I feel so alone." I had just come from a doctoral program at the University of Iowa, surrounded by and a part of a community of students, to being a professor at a university. For the first time in my life, I wasn't a student, and I felt isolated and alone in the new position.

How things changed. I lived in Louisville longer than anyplace in my life, even longer than I'd lived in my hometown.

Earlier in 2014 I distinctly remembered saying to one of my class members at the YMCA, "I will NEVER leave Louisville."

Never say never.

Over those last months before my trip I said many goodbyes. I said goodbye to my lovely little house. I said goodbye to my job at Kentucky Opera. Although I would not miss the job itself, I was going to miss my coworkers and all the talented people I met during those 15 years. I said goodbye to my fabulous and dedicated group fitness class at the YMCA, who would enthusiastically undertake whatever impossible ass-kicking workout I could throw at them and leave with sweaty smiles on their faces and return for more, usually dragging friends and spouses in tow.

I said goodbye to my Derby City CrossFit family. It was my sanctuary and happy place, without which I would have never found my best friend ever and discovered my passion as a coach.

I said goodbye to my VOICES of Kentuckiana family, with whom I had traveled a long, varied, and sometimes rocky road—having served as singer, section leader, board member, board chair, assistant, and guest artistic director. It was heart-wrenching. I cried more the final two weeks than I care to remember, thinking about how much I would miss all those dear to my heart.

I was also saying goodbye to my comfort zones. When I coached, I told people on a daily basis, "Put more weight on the bar! You will NEVER get any stronger until you make yourself lift heavier! You need to push yourself OUT OF YOUR COMFORT ZONE!" I had finally come to realize that the same principle applies to life outside the gym as well.

Yet, throughout my life, I had always played it safe—I was not comfortable with change. I loved my daily routine. It was safe, predictable, and comfortable. But I was really never truly happy. And I would never find happiness or get stronger emotionally and mentally, unless I could push myself out of my comfort zone.

So, I forced myself to do the absolute scariest things I had ever done and pushed out of every single comfort zone I had. I sold the house that was my security blanket. I quit the job that I thought I couldn't do without. I did things that I'd always depended on someone else doing. And I was about to embark on a journey for several months by myself, alone and independent.

I was sad and scared. But at the same time, I felt optimistic and excited. I had absolute faith that having the courage to say goodbye and to let go would lead me to a new and incredible chapter of my life.

The day of that new and incredible chapter had finally arrived. Goodbye Louisville, Kentucky, and hello USA!

CHAPTER 3
Relax, DAMMIT!

The initial stop of my journey was a beautiful lake house in Tennessee belonging to Erin's parents. The house was secluded, quiet, and peaceful, and overlooked a gorgeous turquoise-green lake. It would be the perfect way to start my adventure—relaxing, clearing my mind, and preparing for the journey of a lifetime. However, over those three days I realized what a challenge it was for me to really relax.

The afternoon that I arrived at the house, I settled in. That evening I watched the sunset and stayed up to see the brilliance of a million stars in a pitch-black sky. The next day I rose early and watched a beautiful sunrise. I drank some coffee, went for a walk, did a few hill sprints, and ate breakfast.

After that I decided, "Alright, now it's time to kick back and relax!" I eagerly grabbed *The Noticer* and settled comfortably in an Adirondack chair on the back deck. The book was short and took me no time to read. I took a nap. I journaled about the beginning of my journey. I walked out to the pier by the lake and sat in the hot sun until I couldn't stand it anymore. I jumped into the cold water and paddled around happily for a bit.

After a quick shower, there was still plenty of daylight left, but I felt anxious, as though I had relaxed enough and should now get busy doing one of the many things I'd always done to keep busy: clean the house, mow the lawn, do the laundry. I felt uncomfortable without the structure of a schedule or a list of mundane tasks. Why couldn't I just be lazy and enjoy this time I had with nothing to do? I was on the vacation of a lifetime, for Chrissakes!

* * *

Before I quit my job, I'd kept a furious schedule for years that was jam-packed from the early dawn hours until sometimes 11 p.m. My own workouts and coaching in the morning, my day job, coaching at the Y in the afternoon, and chorus activities and social activities in the evenings took up most of my weekdays and weekends. I very rarely ever "relaxed." My definition of relaxing was doing errands, laundry, yard work, housecleaning, meal prep and cooking, and socializing. I never gave myself the opportunity to be lazy.

I think that in our society the word "lazy" has a really negative connotation to it. The busier you are and the more you do, the more you're worth. We judge ourselves by how busy we are, and we think that if we're not busy, we're not worthwhile. It's a badge of honor to have every moment of our lives occupied.

Being lazy is judged as bad. So, we end up feeling guilty for relaxing and enjoying our own lives. We think, "I should be doing laundry. I should be cleaning the house. I should be organizing that closet that's such a mess," etc. We stop relaxing and start doing. We don't allow ourselves to recharge our batteries. We don't stop and live in the moment of our own lives. We keep ourselves so busy that we never really take time to be comfortable with ourselves.

I kept so incredibly busy that I had no opportunity to really listen to my inner self. I was unhappy and angry and unfulfilled, and didn't know why. It's because I was never still enough to hear that inner voice.

At the lake house, with nothing to do except look deep within my soul, I was able to finally listen to my true self and take responsibility. I was unhappy that I'd lost control of my relationship. I had been unhappy in a job that didn't fulfill my life's purpose of teaching and inspiring others. And I was angry about it. I realized that my anger came from feeling like a victim.

I then thought back over the past several years to every time I'd been angry with my partner, a coworker, or my boss—and that was often. Each time, I realized I felt victimized by people or events. *They* had hurt or wronged me. *They* had been in the wrong. *They* had been unfair to me. I had become very adept at playing the victim. It meant I never had to take responsibility for my own actions. I could just blame others and never change what was making me unhappy.

I had been mad at life for "dealing me this hand," and only then, sitting in that chair looking out at the gorgeous blue-green lake, could I admit that I had been the one holding the deck all along. It was scary and exciting at the same time. Scary because I'd have to get out of my comfort zone and make an effort to finally do something different, but exciting to realize I was not powerless to change my life. In fact, I was in the driver's seat.

CHAPTER 4

A Kindred Spirit

W hen I first started wrapping my head around taking time off for a three-month road trip, I thought of all my horn colleagues from the University of Iowa School of Music who were scattered around the country. I couldn't wait to visit them all. I envisioned the first official stop to be Greensboro, North Carolina, to visit the dearest one of them all, Ab. As I left Tennessee and drove east towards North Carolina, I thought about my old life with my horn.

I started playing the French horn in fourth grade. It came very naturally to me, and I loved it. I had found something that I was really good at and threw myself into it 100%. My mom never had to tell me to practice. In high school, I started taking private lessons, and by junior year I knew I wanted to major in music. After my undergraduate degree, I went to the University of Michigan to get my master's. That was the pinnacle of my horn-playing years. I was surrounded in school with some of the most talented musicians in the country; I was playing gigs with several orchestras around the state and just completely loving my life.

After graduating with a master's, I stayed in Ann Arbor and took on a large studio of private students to go along with my orchestra gigs. That fall, the principal hornist in the Ann Arbor symphony was unavailable for the first concert of the season, so between the rest of the section we shared the principal parts. I was assigned to play principal on a little Milhaud piece. It had an easy little slurry solo, nothing technical at all and in a very easy range. When we started rehearsals, I thought, "Nothing to it—a piece of cake." But something was just not right. I struggled with the simple little solo that a junior high student could have played. I couldn't put my finger on it, but I just couldn't do it. My playing just wasn't easy and natural as it always had been.

All I could think was that I wasn't practicing enough because I was teaching all day long. I practiced more and more, thinking the problem would fix itself, but it didn't get any better. In fact, it got increasingly worse. I became frantic about it, and for the first time ever in my life, I started losing my nerve. Those nerves manifested in a quiver in my lips as I tried to play. Like a total loss of control. I tried with all my might to control it. The harder I tried to control it, the worse it got. I didn't confide in anyone and tried to hide my increasing discomfort and declining performance.

One of my gigs at that time was assistant principal in the Flint Symphony Orchestra. We were performing Brahms Symphony #3, and I was offered the chance to play third horn. I jumped at the opportunity. The third horn part in that particular symphony is beautiful, with a multitude of solos, most of them high, soft, and completely exposed. But as the rehearsals commenced, the pressure I put on myself in the wake of my declining performance started to take its toll. I was surrounded by colleagues with whom I'd played for years at the University of Michigan and who had known me as one of the strongest horn players in the studio. I felt like I had such a high standard to live up to, and the harder I tried to regain any semblance of my past level of playing, the worse it got.

My performance and confidence deteriorated over the span of the rehearsals and not surprisingly culminated in an awful performance. My mind was racing in overdrive with fear through the entire symphony. I was petrified of each approaching solo. Completely overwhelmed with nerves, feeling totally naked, alone and exposed, my whole body shaking along with my lips, I obliterated each solo. It was the worst, most humiliating and embarrassing experience of my life. I felt like I let myself down, I let the conductor down, I let the audience down, I let all my friends and colleagues in the orchestra down. I was completely devastated. It was like a betrayal. The one thing in my life that I had always depended on to make me feel good had deserted me.

My struggles continued over the next several years as I desperately tried everything I could think of to turn things around. I took lessons from teachers around the area, hoping that someone might be able to help, to find out what was wrong and why my lips were quivering. I took several months off, hoping that when I picked my horn back up that the problem had gone away.

Finally, with no place left to turn, I decided to return to school for my doctorate, thinking that playing regularly and studying with a good teacher would bring my playing back. I applied to and was accepted into the doctoral program at the University of Iowa.

I met Ab the summer before my third year at Iowa. I had been the studio teaching assistant the first two years of my doctoral program, and Ab was starting her master's and taking the assistantship over from me. One day that summer, I was in my office practicing when I heard a knock on the door. I opened it up and there stood a beautiful, slender, dark-haired young lady with a wide smile, next to an older woman. She introduced herself as the new TA with the loveliest of Virginia drawls and then turned and introduced her mother. They had come to town to apartment hunt and stopped by the school of music.

I liked Ab immediately. She radiated energy and openness. She was friendly, forthright, and honest. We hit it off and became fast friends. We complemented each other in our horn-playing abilities as well—I was a strong high horn player, and she had the most solid low range and I admired her greatly! Even though my playing had improved somewhat during my doctoral program, I still struggled at times. Ab was a huge source of support for me, encouraging me and helping my confidence tremendously.

My fondest memory of our musical collaboration was of the university symphony's performance of Mahler Symphony #3, one of the longest, most colossal, and horn-heavy symphonies in the classical repertoire. She and I were placed first and second horn, respectively. The symphony was full of first horn solos, and Ab was a calming and reassuring presence next to me throughout the rehearsals and the culminating concert. In the third movement, there is a lovely, lyrical duet between the first and second horn. Our sounds blended beautifully into one lush timbre, and we were totally in tune and in sync. After the utter humiliation of that Brahms 3 performance years earlier, I felt so incredibly grateful to feel some redemption playing one of the most glorious melodies ever written. I really felt like Ab helped me perform to my fullest potential, and I will never forget that performance.

After we left Iowa and went our separate ways, we kept in touch throughout the years. No matter how much time had passed between contact, we picked up as if only days had passed. And, no matter what happened in our lives with our personal relationships or struggles during those years, we completely supported each other with no judgment whatsoever.

At one point, Ab sent me a book she'd read that she thought I would find interesting, *A New Earth* by Eckhart Tolle. It was my first introduction into a spiritual guide to self-improvement. I was intrigued by the concepts of living in the present moment as opposed to dwelling on the past or worrying about the future. Equally intriguing was the description of our ego self, that little voice in our head that takes over our mind with thoughts of negativity, criticism, and judgment.

After gradually giving up playing and teaching horn due to my declining performance, just two years before my big road trip, I drove to Greensboro and gave away my huge library of horn music to Ab's horn studio. During that visit, she spoke to me of her interest in Tao philosophy, the Chinese tradition of living "the way" or living in harmony with the Universe. My friend had taught me a new way to look at life. I couldn't wait to see where we were on our respective paths.

* * *

I arrived in Greensboro to find my dear friend smiling and as vibrant as ever. We caught up on each other's lives and shared a meal and a couple of delightful adult malt beverages at a local microbrewery, The Natty Green. As we sat around the wrought iron table on the patio in the late afternoon sunshine with a gentle blowing breeze, I realized why we could so easily pick up after the years: I had found a kindred spirit.

I shared with her the events leading up to the breakup at the beginning of the year and how devastated I was at the loss of my relationship. Ab comforted me with her belief that everything that happened was exactly as it should be.

She shared some of her own struggles, and I noticed that we both were choosing to look at life and approach our interactions and relationships with others with the same philosophy: accept life as it is that moment and accept others for who they are, without trying to control or change them. I told her what had really helped that spring was my involvement with my community chorus. I explained how excited I'd been conducting them for our 20th anniversary concert; that it had been one of the most fulfilling musical experiences of my life. Me, the horn player who'd never had any training in singing or conducting!

Ab, looking at me knowingly, responded, "Of course you loved it. It's just another vehicle for your musical expression."

I looked at my dear friend with gratitude, and I realized she was right. I'd thought once I stopped playing and teaching horn that I'd lost that part of me forever, but I could still express that part of myself in another way.

Because Ab was scheduled to play a run-out summer concert with the North Carolina Symphony in Kinston, she suggested that after the concert, we could drive to the coast and spend the following day kayaking along the inlets of the Atlantic. What an unexpected surprise! I could hear her play with a fantastic symphony and then get to do one of my favorite, though seldom done, activities.

Thursday afternoon, we loaded the kayaks atop her car and headed east. We arrived at Pearson Park, the outdoor concert venue in Kinston, with plenty of time to spare.

As we walked around the park, we came to the edge of the Neuse River, and there, sitting at a picnic table we encountered a petite, white-haired little old lady. She introduced herself to us as Pinky Harper, 95 going on 96, but we could hardly believe it. She had a twinkle in her eye and a quick wit. She was the epitome of a spry old lady. She told us of her life and all the places that she'd traveled.

We asked her what the secret was to her longevity, and without missing a beat she replied, "Hard work." After that, I almost felt embarrassed to share with her that I'd quit my steady job and was embarking on this adventure that hardly seemed like hard work—but I told her anyway.

Pinky looked me straight in the eye and told me to go for it and not waste a minute of my life.

After the concert, Ab drove us to a little city called Beaufort, just off the North Carolina Coast. We checked in to a lovely little spot called the Inlet Inn. The next morning, we drove across the Atlantic Bridge to Morehead City to watch the sunrise. There had been thunderstorms a few hours earlier, and the sunrise through the remaining clouds was spectacular. The only sound around us was the crash of the waves and the call of the seagulls.

At 8:30 a.m. we loaded our kayaks into the water just off Carrot Island about four miles from the inn. It was already quite warm, but there was a pleasant breeze as we paddled along the inlet. We were headed for Horse Island, hopefully to catch a glimpse of the wild horses that roam the main area of the Rachel Carson Nature Reserve made up of Town Marsh, Carrot Island, Bird Shoal, and Horse Island.

After about an hour of paddling, we turned into an inlet and caught a glimpse of a sole wild horse far off, grazing along the bank. Going a bit farther, we saw two additional horses in the distance.

Satisfied, we headed back the way we'd come, as the sun rose higher and became more intense.

Imagine our stunned surprise when we turned around a bend and came upon an entire herd of wild horses not fifty feet away from us! Hurriedly we grabbed our cameras as they came closer to the bank.

Ab quipped, "Who would've ever thought you'd see wild horses at the ocean?"

Our curiosity satisfied, we paddled back to the boat ramp, exhausted but exhilarated by the experience, loaded the kayaks back onto the car in the blazing heat and humidity, and made our way back to Greensboro.

It is rare in this lifetime to find a friend who loves you for exactly who you are and supports you unconditionally. Who speaks the same language, who is on the same spiritual path, whom I can learn from and who can learn from me. Who enjoys the same activities, with whom you can travel easily and comfortably—with eleventy billion bathroom stops without complaint.

I left my visit with a sense of calm and acceptance that everything up to that point in my life had happened not by accident, but for a reason, even if I didn't know yet what that reason was. I am so thankful for my friend Ab, a true kindred spirit.

CHAPTER 5

A New Friendship with an Old Friend

W hen I contacted another University of Iowa friend, Gretchen, to see if she would mind if I stopped to visit her in Kalamazoo, she told me she would welcome a visit, but not in Kalamazoo. Life opportunities had brought her family to Bethesda, Maryland. How convenient for me—that was just a short drive north from Greensboro.

Ab recommended that I avoid the tried and true I-95 route and suggested that I follow the less-traveled I-29 instead. It was great advice. Virginia was beautiful—rolling hills, mountains, green as far as the eye could see.

I arrived in Bethesda, a beautiful city just north of Washington, DC, and pulled in in front of a 17-floor high-rise. Gretchen, her husband Tim, their 7-year old daughter, Iola, and their adorable dog, Sushi, came down to lead me to the parking garage. Gretchen, sporting an adorable pixie haircut, looked as young as when we were in school together.

* * *

Way back when Gretchen and I had first met, she was a college freshman, and I was in the second year of my DMA program. There was about a 13-year age difference between us. I remember that although much younger than I, Gretchen possessed a quiet maturity and an appealing gentle spirit not common in most 18-year-olds. Plus, I was just flat-out in awe of her natural musicality expressed on her horn. Her playing appeared effortless, and in light of my own struggles, I admired that. It's no surprise that we were friends back in school.

After I graduated and moved to my position in Louisville and she to a master's program at Western Michigan, our paths had crossed only twice, once in 1999 at the International Horn Symposium in Athens, Georgia, and then in 2001 at the Symposium in Kalamazoo. In Athens, I'd met her boyfriend Tim, a tuba player she'd met at WMU. The three of us had hung out together during that week. I remembered in particular going out to dinner at a wonderful Italian restaurant and having a very comfortable time with them, getting to know

Gretchen more as a peer, and feeling totally at ease with Tim, who was a really great guy and easy to get to know. In Kalamazoo, we'd reconnected again, and this time they'd just been married.

After that, Tim went on to law school, and Gretchen had a very successful freelance orchestral career and a lot of adjunct teaching. Tim got a position in Chicago, they moved twice while they were there and had Iola, and Gretchen left playing and teaching. Shortly after that, Gretchen went through a major medical crisis—a severe blood clot in her aorta causing clots in other parts of her body. It was a frightening time for all of them, but fortunately she recovered.

After that scare, Tim decided to slow down so that they could spend more time together, and he found a position back in Kalamazoo where they'd met. A few years after that, they moved to Bethesda. Because of the damage from the surgery, Gretchen had also stopped playing her horn professionally, which was painful for her, as it had been for me.

* * *

Although several years had passed since I'd last seen her, we picked up as if no time at all had gone by. After a few margaritas and a delicious dinner at one of their favorite Mexican restaurants, Gringos and Mariachis, we headed back to the apartment and up to the rooftop pool with Iola. Having had such a tough time with my partner's children, I had been just a bit anxious about meeting Iola, but she took to me immediately. We bonded by making a fort out of beach towels and pool furniture.

That evening, Gretchen and I settled ourselves at the rooftop lounge, where we talked for hours about our lives and the unexpected twists and turns that they'd taken. I shared how difficult it had been for me to give up playing and teaching after devoting most of my life to it. I realized that I had based my whole self-worth on what came out of the end of my horn, and I had to learn to feel worthy for just being me.

Gretchen sympathized, relating her own pain that playing wasn't a part of her life anymore. Her horn playing had given her such joy, but after her sudden unexpected health scare, frightened to have her life end in a moment, things were put into perspective. She was grateful to be alive, living a fulfilling life with her husband and daughter.

We both agreed: life brings you exactly to the place you are meant to be at the very moment.

The next morning, the sun rose early, as did Iola, who without any shyness or trepidation whatsoever jumped onto my bed with the little dog Sushi and promptly serenaded me with a song on her harmonica. I was really touched that this adorable little girl liked me so much. I asked her if I could try to play it. I gave it a whirl and made it an absolute priority to find one for myself.

Gretchen and I had something else in common: she had also become active in CrossFit in the past couple of years. Tough Temple CrossFit was located almost directly across the street from her apartment, and we made plans to go there that morning for a workout.

We had a healthy light breakfast, highlighted by a couple of shots of delicious espresso. I'm a true coffee fiend, and I was fascinated by her Nespresso maker. We changed into our workout clothes and walked over to the gym for our workout. Some unconventional coaching notwithstanding, the workout of heavy front squats and inverted rows challenged us both immensely. Although I have wonderful memories of playing the horn next to Gretchen, I really enjoyed this new experience of working out alongside my friend.

That evening, after Tim returned from work, we made preparations for dinner on the rooftop patio. Tim offered me a drink from his collection of fine single malt scotch. I balked just a bit; since living in Kentucky the past 17 years, I'd attained a love and appreciation for fine bourbon. I told him my only experience with scotch had been my mom's scotch and soda. I was reticent to try something I didn't think I'd really like.

Tim laughed and said single malt scotch was an entirely different thing. Excitedly, almost like a little kid, he selected four fine scotches from his collection, and we had a little tasting. I was impressed by his knowledge of the different qualities of each bottle. After sampling each one, I decided on my favorite—Lagavulin, a 16-year-old scotch that had been aged in a smoky barrel, resulting in an equally smoky, unique taste. I was proud of myself for being open to trying something new.

After our cocktail hour, we gathered up the makings for dinner and headed up to the rooftop again. I watched over Iola as she swam while Tim and Gretchen prepared steaks and veggies on the rooftop grills. Once it was ready, we enjoyed the delicious meal with an exquisite bottle of red wine as the sun set over the city.

Our conversation veered towards our mutual love of music, the French horn, and Mahler symphonies. Tim quickly obliged us and set Spotify to the slow movement of Mahler 6. We sat in this idyllic setting listening to the hauntingly beautiful horn solos in the symphony and reminisced about our own horn-playing days, including that Mahler 3 performance back at the University of Iowa. The evening could not have been more perfect.

It was absolutely incredible to me to reconnect and rediscover our many common interests and mutual core beliefs, most of which we'd never discussed so many years ago: our love of music, our experiences with the horn, our love of teaching, our passions for fitness, CrossFit, and real food, each of our life's journeys, and the challenges which had been presented to us and how we'd faced those challenges.

When I marveled aloud at the similarities in our priorities and spiritual paths and the ease of our friendship despite the span of years, Gretchen uttered a simple yet profound statement: "When there is a connection, time is irrelevant."

On the phone later that evening, I remarked to a friend how grateful I was that my visits with my old friends had been filled with such meaningful conversations. And she remarked, "Kindred spirits abound when you are open to the Universe." True words and I promised to stay open to the Universe on this adventure.

CHAPTER 6

Think I'll Go Down to the Coast for a While

On my last morning in Bethesda, I quickly looked at my map to estimate where I might end up that evening. Myrtle Beach seemed like it might be too crowded and Georgetown looked dull, but Pawley's Island, located between the two, sounded quaint, very casual, and appealing.

I said goodbye to Gretchen around 10 a.m., and drove onto I-95 to get to my destination as quickly as possible. Well, as they say, the best-laid plans . . . It was not to be. Construction, as far as the eye could see, turned I-95 into a parking lot. Normally that would have irritated the hell out of me, but I was trying to look at life in a new way. I used the situation as an exercise in letting go of control, and patiently crept along.

Eventually, I made my way to Route 1 and headed south. The trip took much longer than I'd anticipated, but I was on no schedule whatsoever. I arrived on Pawley's Island around 7 p.m., very hot and tired. Upon checking into the hotel, I realized that I had not done enough research. It was old and worn and dark—but at least it was clean.

The upside of the hotel was that it was barely a mile and a half from beach access. I could hardly contain my excitement. A few months before my trip, I'd discovered a song by Eliza Gilkyson called "Coast." I'd been struck by the lovely acoustic melody, but especially by the lyrics.

Think I'll go down to the coast for a while,
Find a little cabin by the sea.
Think I need to be alone for a while,
Find out what ever became of me.

Think I'll go down to the sea for awhile,
kick my shoes off in the sand.
Don't know what I'm gonna be for a while,
don't want to try to understand.

For some reason, I longed to be on as many beaches as I could. I thought perhaps that sitting on the sand, looking out onto the ocean, staring into the sun, that somehow, I could connect to the Universe and find an answer to my unhappiness, an answer for my restlessness; that I would find the meaning of my life. I was going to take any chance I could to visit the seashore, and I promised myself that I would dip my feet into the Atlantic Ocean, the Gulf of Mexico, and the Pacific Ocean.

I scoped out the location, found a perfect parking spot right next to the beach access, and strolled onto the beach. Omigosh it was charming, clean, and uncrowded. The evening was balmy and breezy, and the Atlantic waves crashed gently onto the shore. I walked into the water up to my knees; it was warm and the waves softly caressed my legs. I wandered up and down the beach for an hour, my feet leaving footprints that were quickly erased by the waves. I stared out over the horizon, thinking of the song I'd come to love so much. Waiting for anything to come to me from the Universe. But my mind was tired, my body was tired. Perhaps the next day. I eagerly looked forward to the next morning and what I was certain would be an incredible sunrise. With darkness quickly approaching, I made my way back to the worn Motel 6.

I woke a half hour earlier than my alarm was set for, still used to my early rising. I packed up my camera, beach towel, and beach chair, drove to the same little parking spot, and cautiously made my way in the pitch black to the beach. Flashlight in hand, I set my little beach chair up in the darkness and settled in with my camera and waited.

Slowly the sky began to lighten, from dark blue to pink to orange. A movement right next to me startled me—a little white dog was sniffing at the back of my chair. Attached to the little dog at the other end of the leash was an older woman; we exchanged a quiet good morning as she and her pup walked towards the beach. Other beach-lovers appeared, walking, jogging, enjoying the quiet morning as was I. The clouds filtered the sunrise, and it finally broke over the horizon at around 6:15 in a glowing red sphere. It was one of the most beautiful sunrises I'd ever seen.

* * *

The next stop on my Amazing Adventure was the historic city of Charleston. As I approached the city, a huge bridge loomed in front of me. I felt a tightness in the pit of my stomach the closer I got to it. When I was growing up, my grandfather lived in South Chicago. To get there, we'd take the Chicago Skyway and cross a gigantic bridge that for some reason always scared me to death. I still remember the feeling of vertigo that I'd get as we approached it. Perhaps that's when my fear of heights started.

Feeling almost the same dizziness, I crossed over the huge scary bridge into Charleston, drove down to Murray Boulevard, parked my car, and walked along the harbor. After a few blocks, I arrived at White Point Garden. I sat near a quaint gazebo in the center of the park and enjoyed the cool shade before heading back to my car.

After about an hour and a half, I crossed yet another stomach-lurching bridge into Savannah, Georgia. I arrived at my hotel and was pleasantly surprised to discover that despite its outward shabby appearance, my room was much improved over the tired old Motel 6 on Pawley's Island.

Feeling hungry, I looked up suggestions for casual local dinner and noticed several recommendations for Crystal Beer Parlor. I drove several miles until I arrived at a very non-descript-looking building. Inside, however, it was PACKED with a lively Friday night crowd.

Somewhat apprehensively, I walked in among the throngs of people. I'd never been very comfortable among a crowd of strangers, so going out to eat by myself was going to be something I had to get used to over the next few months. It would have been easy to just pick up some dinner and bring it back to the safe and comfortable confines of my hotel room, but this trip was all about facing my fears and opening myself up to the world.

I took a deep breath to quell the tiny knot of anxiety in my stomach and walked in towards the massive wooden bar. Smack dab in the middle of the crowded bar would have challenged my comfort zone too much, and all the way on the end felt like I'd be isolating myself. So, I chose a seat halfway between the middle and the left side, nodded toward the bartender, and asked him for some kind of a chocolaty porter.

He brought me the most delicious coffee stout, and as I sat there, slowly allowing myself to relax into the moment, the most wonderful wave of giddy happiness overcame me. I almost felt as if I was high. I felt truly alive for the first time in my life. I can't explain why, other than I was so grateful to have the means to be on this adventure. I couldn't stop smiling as I took in everything around me, the friendly, bustling bar and wait staff, the Friday night crowd, the rich flavor of the beer. I felt free and totally at peace. Could it be that just opening myself up and chipping away at the wall of insecurity was the answer to some of my unhappiness? At that moment, it seemed to be true.

The following morning, I thought I would hit the Savannah riverfront before heading out. I found a parking spot right on Bay Street and walked down the uneven brick sidewalk to the stairs down to River Street and the waterfront.

I spent about an hour walking around the beautiful homes a few blocks away from the riverfront. I had no idea where I was going, but ended up exactly where I'd hoped, in front of the Mercer House, featured in the fantastic book, *Midnight in the Garden of Good and Evil*. It's amazing how when you open yourself up to the present moment, you come upon exactly what you hoped for without exactly intending to.

CHAPTER 7
Vulnerability

I love CrossFit. I joined Derby City CrossFit in February of 2010 and never looked back. It was one of the best things that ever happened to me. I was fitter than I'd ever been in my life, I'd made some of the best friends I'd ever had, and it made me aware of my true calling. It also offered a fantastic community no matter where you were. CrossFit is like a common language, and in speaking this language you're friends just by knowing it.

A year or so previously, a woman participated in our class at DCCF over several months. Her job required her to stay in various cities for a period of time, and we were lucky to have her join our gym and work out with us. Jody was quiet and no-nonsense and extremely strong. Her home base was Florida, and she had posted some pictures on Facebook of a stunning view of an inlet just off the backyard of her house. When I commented to her on how lovely and serene it looked, she replied, "Hey, if you're ever down there, come on and see me."

When I started my adventure, I messaged her just a bit nervously and said I'd be in the area and would love to visit. I almost felt like I was inviting myself! But she responded immediately, "Of course you must stay with me!"

Since the time she'd been in Louisville, she had started building a new house and also opened her own CrossFit gym! Her regular gym down there had recently closed, and since there was no other affiliate close by, she decided to take her own "leap of faith" and open one herself! I couldn't wait to spend some time with her and work out at the new box.

That weekend, her CrossFit affiliate was participating in a competition in Daytona Beach, so I made the short three-hour drive from Savannah to the Ocean Center in Daytona. I arrived just in time to see the last workout of the day in which two of her members were competing.

After cheering them on, we headed back to her beautiful home in the charming Palm Coast area. I was a tiny bit anxious about the next couple of days. Although Jody and I had been in the same morning class for several months, we really didn't know each other that well, and here I was about to spend a couple of days with her.

In the past, I might have given into what I would have called my "shyness" and never even reached out to her. But as I spent that spring and summer looking closely at myself, I realized that it wasn't shyness, it was fear—fear of being vulnerable and letting others get to know me. I guess it was a fear of them not liking me. It's safer and more comfortable never reaching out, because then you can't be rejected, right? I was determined to dispel that limiting belief and breach my comfort zone.

Jody put any of my anxiety to rest. She was a perfect host. Upon entering her beautiful home, she offered me a drink, a fantastic single malt scotch, Macallan's 12-year. I eagerly accepted, excited to have another opportunity to appreciate this new drink. I felt no awkwardness whatsoever as we easily talked about the success of her new CrossFit gym and the plans for her new home she was building. I enjoyed getting to know her better.

Jody was very exacting about her nutrition and followed a strict Paleo diet—fruits, vegetables, lean meats and seafood, nuts, seeds, and healthy fats. She was a great cook as well and fixed a wonderful meal of grass-fed burgers, a fantastic slaw made with apple cider vinegar and coconut oil, and fresh fruit. Dessert rivaled any restaurant's: cacao powder, coconut oil, crushed walnuts, and finely chopped cherries, spread out on foil and set in the refrigerator. It was fantastic!

Sunday morning, we rose at about 6:30 a.m. and drank some strong coffee in preparation for the CrossFit "church service," which that day just happened to be one of the toughest Hero WODS imaginable: Badger, consisting of 3 rounds of 30 squat cleans, 30 pull-ups, and an 800-meter run.

At 8 a.m. on a Sunday morning, after a weekend of competition, 13 CrossFit BearCat members showed up, ready to take on the WOD (workout of the day)—in 90-degree-plus weather. I'd done Badger twice before, but never at the prescribed weight of 65 pounds. I was determined to use that, even if it meant that I could not complete the full three rounds within the 35-minute time cap. It would have been easy to use a lighter weight and get through the workout more quickly and easily, and really, would anyone notice? But I remembered my mantra from the inception of this adventure: get out of my comfort zone. And I thought of my own words to my own class members: "You never get stronger if you don't put more weight on the bar."

I struggled mightily, especially in the brutal heat. Class members who had already finished carried out the CrossFit tradition of cheering on those who had yet to finish. Complete strangers urged me on, using my name, pulling for every rep I could muster. I completed two full rounds and 8 squat cleans of the final round before the time expired. It pretty much crushed me, but at least I wasn't alone. I was grateful to the fantastic supportive community at CrossFit BearCat.

Later that day, Jody and I headed to downtown Flagler Beach, a quaint little town right on the Atlantic. It was interesting driving into town. Because of some zoning restrictions, there were no high buildings at all on the waterfront, so the ocean was fully visible as we drove towards the beach. We stopped at a local winery to have a refreshing adult beverage, and while chatting up the owner about the competition that weekend, a young girl behind the counter overheard us talking and walked over. She introduced herself as Sara, and started talking CrossFit. It turned out that she was a highly-skilled and experienced Olympic lifter, exactly the type Jody had been looking for to provide some quality Olympic lift coaching at BearCat CrossFit! Sara had been hoping to find an opportunity to coach at a CrossFit gym. How fortuitous that we'd just happened to stop by that day. I shook my head almost in disbelief.

I'd been listening to a Wayne Dyer CD on the road recently, *There's a Spiritual Solution to Every Problem*, in which he stated emphatically, "There are no coincidences," meaning that the Universe works to arrange things perfectly. I thought to myself that this situation was a perfect example of what he had been talking about.

* * *

I considered myself very fortunate on the trip so far. I'd been gone for only two weeks, yet in that time I'd reconnected with some friends from all walks of my life. I appreciated my visit with Jody for several reasons. I was proud that I'd expanded out of my safe cocoon of solitude in order to spend a couple of days with someone I barely knew and to get to know her and her own leap of faith. I took a chance at her gym to open myself to others and to challenge myself more than I'd ever been willing to in that workout. Our mutual love of CrossFit enabled me to do that. I was slowly learning to open my heart and share my life challenges and insecurities with friends. By taking that courageous step, they'd in turn shared their hearts with me. In doing so, I was gradually realizing an important lesson: the Universe acts as a boomerang—what you give out you get in return.

CHAPTER 8
Familiar But Oh-So-Different

L eesburg, Florida was on my map from the beginning of my plan. My very favorite aunt (Mama's oldest sister) and uncle had lived there for 23 years, and I visited them every time I was ever in Florida. Aunt Pat was 92 and in the spring of 2014 had fallen into some very bad health. I was desperately hopeful that she'd still be healthy when I traveled to Florida, but it was not to be. She passed away early in May, peacefully and in the wonderful care of hospice.

Growing up, Aunt Pat and Uncle Bern lived in a lovely little brick house on the South Side of Chicago. Uncle Bern inherited the house from his uncle. I still remember the address: 11050 Avenue C. They had no children of their own.

As a child, I was terrified of Aunt Pat. She was an intimidating and stern presence to me, always impeccably dressed and accessorized, and very particular about her house and belongings. My brothers, who are older than I, had a much different relationship with our aunt and uncle, and I was envious of the friendship they had.

As I grew older, that fear quickly dissipated as I realized that Aunt Pat was the furthest thing from scary. She was one of the kindest, most generous and loving people I'd ever been lucky enough to know. She and Uncle Bern attended most of my graduations, recitals, and other milestone events through the years. When my ex Patti and I were together, we traveled to Florida once or twice a year, and always made a point to visit them. One year we made plans to visit Aunt Pat and Uncle Bern and then surprised them by bringing my sister Renée along. Mama and I traveled down together for a visit in 2009. In 2013 when I'd been vacationing in the Orlando area, I drove up to Leesburg for a wonderful visit, which turned out to be the last time I would see Aunt Pat.

Aunt Pat had not had an easy life growing up. My grandfather kicked her out of the house when she was just 16, and she had to make it on her own. Her first job was in a chili parlor right there on the East Side of Chicago. She continued to support herself as a waitress and then worked as a "26 girl." Twenty-six was a dice game that originated in Chicago; 26 girls rolled the dice and kept score. She worked in the very affluent Hyde Park neighborhood at a club called Buzz's, so many of her customers were wealthy businessmen. Aunt Pat, who my mom always said was no dummy, would listen to the business chitchat among these men and ask what they were talking about. They told her they were playing the stock market, and she responded, "Well, tell me how you play it." They did, and Aunt Pat quickly caught on and subsequently showed quite a knack for picking stocks, doing quite well for herself!

As a young man, Uncle Bernie was one of the strong muscle men who would work out on the beach on the Chicago lakefront. My mom, a swimmer, often had practice at the lakefront, and there she met Uncle Bern. They had a mutual interest in working out and dated a couple of times before deciding just to be friends. After that, Uncle Bern went out with Aunt Ali, the middle sister! I think it was at this time he went overseas to serve our country. He served as a paratrooper, who, because of his dangerous profession, was paid $50 for every jump. He had always wanted a car, so when he returned from the war, he bought himself a black Cadillac with his war earnings.

One day after returning from the service, he just happened to go to the bar at which Aunt Pat was working. Everyone was still under the impression that he was dating Aunt Ali, but he said, "Nope, not anymore." Apparently, he and Aunt Pat had hit it off, and thus began one of the longest, most loving marriages I'd ever seen, 60 or so years strong.

Aunt Pat and Uncle Bern worshiped each other. I never witnessed anything but loving devotion on both parts. Never a cross word, never anything but love and respect. Aunt Pat told me that the secret to a long, loving, healthy relationship was trust. She said, "You have to have trust."

Aunt Pat had pet names for all of the girls in her family—her sisters and nieces. Mine was Sweetface. I can still hear her saying that to me now, "Hi Sweetface!" in her unique voice. Thanks to the wonders of smartphones, I saved several of my voicemails from her, so I could hear her say, "Hi Sweetface!" anytime I wanted.

When she'd write me, she'd draw a little smiley face right next to Sweetface, and when I'd write her, I'd sign "Sweetface" with a smiley face and a heart.

Aunt Pat had the most unique handwriting, to say the least. It was beautiful, but extremely difficult to decipher! Even as an adult, I would read her letters very slowly and out loud, trying to make out her intricate cursive. My mom was pretty adept— she could read Aunt Pat's writing at a normal speed, without any slow sounding out. Aunt Pat's letters and cards would be filled with tiny, shiny graffiti-like confetti. Until I got used to it and remembered in advance, I'd pull her card or letter out of the envelope and spill its shiny confetti bits all over the place, and then kick myself! Aunt Pat got me!

Aunt Pat loved cashmere—cashmere sweaters, cardigans, tees, turtlenecks. Her drawers and closets were filled with cashmere. Uncle Bern called their house "The House of Cashmere." You'd think that cashmere would be quite non-essential since they lived in Florida, but Aunt Pat was always cold, and I'm sure the cashmere felt great in the ever-present Florida air-conditioning. From time to time through the years, she'd have no more need of certain sweaters, and she'd send some to me. They were beautiful, and they always smelled of her signature perfume, Opium. I cherish them all to this day.

When Aunt Pat and Uncle Bern moved to Florida years ago, they became very involved with the Ice House, a community theatre in nearby Mt. Dora. Uncle Bern has worked as a carpenter there to this day, assisting with building the sets. He has been recognized by the Ice House many times and even has appeared onstage for some performances!

Through the years and through many an artistic director, they remained loyal and supportive to this theater, and are beloved by the local community. Ah, that reminds me of an important story—Aunt Pat did not like her given name, Grace. She had it legally changed to Patricia when she became an adult. When she moved down to Florida, she became known as Trish to all those there.

Throughout my adult years, my relationship with Aunt Pat grew closer and closer. Through many trials and tribulations of life, including those of my career and relationship challenges, I would call Aunt Pat and pour out my heart and soul to her. She would listen as only Aunt Pat could, and lovingly yet assertively give me sage advice, whether I was ready to hear it or not. Over the past ten years or so, I realized that despite a large age difference, she had become one of my closest friends.

* * *

The week my adventure brought me to Leesburg, Florida, in turning into the subdivision of Aunt Pat and Uncle Bern's home for probably the fifteenth time in the past 23 years, it hit me hard that this time, she would not be there. Overcome with emotion, I pulled over in tears. After several minutes, I gathered myself and pulled into the driveway of their home.

Uncle Bern opened the door with a big smile and sporting his ever-present scruffy beard. I walked in, and the smell of Aunt Pat's perfume still filled the house. It felt like at any moment she'd walk out of her bedroom and into the room. I brought my bags into her bedroom; everything was just as she'd left it.

Uncle Bern came in, and he showed me her handwritten note with detailed instructions of which belongings to leave her loved ones. She left me a beautiful emerald ring, a lovely yellow jade necklace and matching bracelet, and her baby locket.

Uncle Bern and I picked out a few more cashmere sweaters for me, so I set those aside with the little bags of cloves that keep the moths at bay. He offered to give me anything else I liked, and I desperately wanted to take every single thing there—every sweater she'd ever worn, every purse she'd ever carried, every bracelet she'd ever worn, her perfume, her lotion, her little books, her collection of turtles, her writing accessories—as if that alone would keep Aunt Pat with me. But it was not the material things that I needed. It was the legacy of her love and generosity and kindness that I would keep in my heart by which to remember her.

* * *

The rest of my two-day visit with Uncle Bern was wonderful. We went to the Ice House and I met Darlin, the artistic director, who was busy planning July's production. I met David, the set designer, and his little dog, Patrick Murphy. Uncle Bern gave me a tour of the newly remodeled lobby, brought me backstage, and proudly showed me the production set in progress.

We went out to eat, we watched tennis and old movies together, we looked at old pictures, and he told me numerous stories about the past. He admitted that it was hard for him, especially when he got up in the morning and Aunt Pat was not there, and when he got home from the theater at night to the empty house. He often stayed later and later at the theater, watching the rehearsals in the evening, even though he quipped to me, "You know rehearsals are like watching the grass grow." I'm grateful to Darlin for giving him the opportunity to stay involved and busy.

When I left, I hugged his still-strong but very thin frame as hard as I could. I struggled with every bit of my will to keep my tears from spilling over, trying to stay positive and strong and hopefully giving him strength as well. I told him how much I'd enjoyed the visit and reassured him that my travels would be safe and that everything in my life was going to work out as it should.

I drove away, carrying with me the mementos Aunt Pat had left me, along with the treasured memories of my most beloved aunt.

CHAPTER 9
Papa

A fter spending the next couple of days relaxing on the beach in Clearwater, I started my way west.

I left at around 6 a.m. in search of coffee just as the dawn emerged over the horizon. The sky was a deep azure, and for the first time that summer, it was deliciously cool. My car thermometer indicated a refreshing 61 degrees outside. I found a Starbucks and as I pulled up to the drive-thru counter, I remarked to the young barista, "Omigosh, what a gorgeous morning!"

She replied, "Yes, it's such a relief!"

With a nice big cup of steaming coffee in hand, I headed west on Interstate 10 towards New Orleans. It was peaceful and quiet on the road as the sun started its ascent into the crystal clear blue summer sky behind me. As I enjoyed the solitude of the early morning drive, my thoughts wandered to my dad.

Papa was a quiet man, very gentle and kind. He'd give you the shirt off of his back if you needed it. He possessed many creative talents—as a young man he sketched and painted and wrote stories. I remember that he kept them in a big manila envelope in the bottom drawer of the huge desk in his study. My siblings and I would take them out from time to time and look with amazement at his macabre but creative cartoons and accompanying stories. He had a beautiful singing voice, and one of my fondest and most cherished memories was of him singing "Waltzing Matilda" to me and my little sister at bedtime. He loved poetry, and at other bedtimes he would recite in his rich voice the ghastly poem, "The Cremation of Sam McGee."

Papa wasn't outwardly emotional nor did he express his love in so many words, but he was always there for me as I grew up, helping with homework, attending all my horn recitals, taking me and a carload of my stuff back and forth to college each year, or loading me and my cat and belongings into a trailer to take me to a new city. Once I moved away from home for good and came back to visit, he'd always reach into his shirt pocket and hand me a fifty-dollar bill "for gas" as I got into my car to leave. I'm convinced he did everything that he could to show his family how much he cared for us despite his inability to be really emotionally available. It was like he had a wall around that part of himself.

Papa worked for Northern Illinois Gas Company for his entire working life, from about the age of 16. To this day it's still kind of a mystery to me what he did. I know he was a "rate man," and from what my mom told me he was very good at his job. My mom told me that twice he was offered the chance to move to either Atlanta or New York City for positions with different utility companies, but he never accepted. None of us knew why he didn't.

At night, my dad would come home from work, and my mom would have a martini ready for him in the freezer. Gin martini with olives and onions. After dinner, while we watched TV as a family, he'd have a couple of beers and oftentimes nod off. When you grow up with this, you accept it as normal. My dad never acted drunk or was violent or abusive, and it was never discussed. However, as I grew older, I realized that my dad had a drinking problem. What drove him to drink and move deeper and deeper into himself, I'll never know. He didn't discuss it with me, any of my siblings, or my mom. All I can guess is that he must have been terribly unhappy or frustrated with something in his life. I know without a doubt he loved his family; but I have no idea what demons he grew up with or what he had to deal with every day at work that might have caused his unhappiness. His drinking and smoking contributed to the gradual decline in his health, leading to cancer, several small strokes, chronic obstructive pulmonary disease, and ultimately to his death in 2006.

As I reflected on all that as I drove that early morning, I thought back to the past 15 years and how I felt unhappy, unfulfilled, and trapped in my job. I'd settled for it because it was safe and secure—I had health insurance, I could keep paying my mortgage, and I was under the false belief that if I left I would be unable to get any other job. It seemed safer to me to stay unhappy rather than take a risk and leave it.

As I thought about this, I realized that maybe this was how Papa had lived—staying with his position, never accepting those opportunities in Atlanta or New York City, perhaps because "the devil you know is better than the one you don't know." Or perhaps he was under the false belief that he shouldn't uproot his family and disrupt our lives in order to relocate. Or perhaps he was overcome by the fear of the repercussions if it didn't work out, so he settled for the job he had because it was safe and secure.

Although fortunately I have never developed a drinking problem like my dad, I developed many unhealthy behaviors and habits, which gave me a feeling of supposed control in my life. All my work, activities, coaching, and meticulous schedule had kept my fears, feelings, and the discontent of settling for an unhappy life smothered and out of sight.

* * *

Then it hit me—although everyone in my life had told me I'm so much like my mom (I look like her, have many of her same mannerisms, and much of the same temperament), I actually take after my dad in many ways as well.

I was overcome with gratefulness for finally having the courage to admit I was unhappy and admit that I alone had the power to change that.

And there, as I drove along the interstate that beautiful morning, I cried—for my dad and his pain, and for my courage to let go, take a huge leap of faith, leave my unhappiness behind, and not continue to live with the same kind of pain that had befallen my dad.

CHAPTER 10
Reunited in the Big Easy

New Orleans—the city of fantastic food and even better music. I couldn't wait to spend a few days in the Big Easy. My last visit had been about 10 years ago, and I was eager to come back and enjoy the city again. Only I wouldn't be alone . . .

Back at the lake house in TN, while reflecting on the past several months and after an honest examination and accounting of my actions, I reached out to Kat, my ex. I sent her a letter in which I released the past and all my hurt, and thanked her for what we'd shared for so many years. She texted back her appreciation for me reaching out, and over the next few weeks we tentatively started communicating with each other.

In kind of a "postmortem" we looked back upon the relationship, and I took responsibility for my part in its demise. Perhaps it was the distance that had separated us or the work I was doing on myself, but I found myself being able to be more honest and vulnerable with her than I'd been able to when we were together. Finally, we both admitted that we still loved each other but just left it at that.

When I told her I would be going through New Orleans, a city she'd never visited, she said, "Wouldn't it be great if we could be there together?" I told her I would love to have her join me there. So, she made the arrangements for time off, and we planned to spend a few days together. I was overjoyed. I'd spent months and months in such grief over the breakup, and now in a few days we would be reunited! My heart was singing every moment of the day.

I made arrangements to stay at a little bed and breakfast that I'd stayed in on my first visit, Elysian Fields, located just a few blocks east of the French Quarter on Elysian Fields Avenue. It wasn't available until the day after we'd planned to arrive, so I booked a room in Baton Rouge for the night.

I arrived before Kat did, and waited with my heart pounding. It had been a couple of months since I'd last seen her, and I had missed her tremendously. When I saw her pull into the parking lot, I walked out to her car to meet her. My heart leapt in my chest as I saw her beautiful smile. Tears were in my eyes as we hugged each other, and I felt like all was well in the world in the embrace of her arms. We spent the rest of the evening in deep conversations about our feelings for each other and how even after the breakup and months apart, we still truly loved each other.

The next day, we headed towards New Orleans. We arrived around 1 p.m. and pulled up right in front of the inn. It looked like it hadn't changed a bit. We brought our belongings up to the room and then headed down the street just a few blocks until we saw a great little brunch spot, the Ruby Slipper. I put my name in for a short wait, and we enjoyed a little mimosa-like concoction from the bar. We enjoyed our lunch together as if we had been on our first date, all smiles and fluttery stomachs.

After lunch, we headed towards the French Quarter via Frenchmen Street. Kat, who has a keen appreciation for the New Orleans music tradition, was thrilled to see the many little bars and clubs lining the street, and could not wait to hear the live music later in the evening. We walked through the many stalls at the French Market, browsing the jewelry, masks, and other wares. It was blazing hot and very crowded as we walked along the quarter, hand in hand, in and out of the little voodoo and gift shops.

The heat was quite unbearable, even for me, so we walked back to Elysian Fields for a mid-day nap. That evening, we grabbed a quick bite to eat and then we were ready to hear some music. We wandered down Frenchmen Street, music streaming out of all the little clubs, and then picked out a trumpet playing from the inside of a little Japanese bar. We wandered in and settled at the bar, listening to a petite woman playing along with a pianist, bass, and drums.

Although she was very talented, as they continued to play, we became enthralled by the pianist. I have never in my life heard such unbelievable jazz piano playing. He was spectacular. Chart after chart, he jammed away, exhibiting unbelievable technique and the most incredible improvisation

I've ever heard. We looked around and shook our heads; the bar was practically empty, and this kind of talent deserved a packed house.

The combo finished the set after about an hour. We walked out of the bar and noticed a crowd gathering on the corner right across from our dinner spot at the Praline Connection. We saw a band forming of about ten boys, teenagers mostly. The group consisted of a couple of drums, a tuba, about three trombones, and four trumpets. The young men began to play, and they were phenomenal. Real New Orleans brass band stuff. The different instruments took turns playing solos, and they played on and on, with no breaks at all. Their endurance was remarkable.

An older woman was in front, watching over them and directing them from time to time. She began to dance and play along with a tambourine. The crowd clapped, whooped with enthusiasm, and cheered them along. When they finally took a break, she addressed the crowd and implored us to keep in mind that for every dollar bill thrown into the donation box, it was split equally, and each boy would receive ten cents of that dollar. In my mind, judging by the quality of the performance they had just given, they should have received hundreds of dollars each.

As the night grew late, we wandered over to a charming artist colony along a little corridor, brightly lit with white Christmas lights. It felt so romantic and intimate, set apart in some way. The stalls were decorated with unique jewelry, wooden goods, and other types of art. The sidewalks were covered with colorful chalk messages left by the tourists ambling in and out of the corridor. Seeing a bucket filled with sidewalk chalk, I chose a piece and drew a heart with our initials in it. We hugged and smiled at each other as we left the little colony.

We slowly returned to the inn in the thick evening air and sat out on the front patio balcony, recapping all the wonderful music we'd heard that evening. We basked in each other's company, enjoying the balmy New Orleans breeze and the sounds of the late night: far off music, street noise, and the cicadas and other night creatures. In my mind, the day could not have been more perfect.

Late the next morning, we enjoyed a hearty breakfast and then excitedly headed in the direction of Bourbon Street. It was almost noon, and shops just started to open up. We turned on St. Ann Street and headed south towards Cafe du Monde. Walking down Prisoners Alley we passed some extraordinary displays of art—paintings, charcoal drawings, prints, and etchings created by local artists. Kat was enthralled. She engaged each artist in conversation, discovering their inspiration for their creations. She picked out several charcoal drawings to bring back home with her.

New Orleans seems to go into nap mode around 4 p.m. We relaxed at the inn; then around 7 we dressed to go out for one more evening. Kat and I headed to Cafe Negril, a brightly-lit little club just a few doors down. The band that night consisted of drums, bass, electric guitar, keyboard, and a fantastic harmonica player. We were excited to hear that anyone could sign up and play a set with the band. We settled ourselves in a back corner of the bar, and I leaned into the crook of Kat's arm, feeling safe and loved as we lost ourselves in the music of New Orleans.

After a couple of hours, we started to make our way back to the inn. As we walked down the sidewalk, Kat noticed a little tattoo parlor—still open and it was almost midnight! She looked at me with a mischievous smile and beckoned me in with her.

"C'mon! I want to get a memento of our trip!"

I was astounded. "You're kidding! It's almost midnight!"

She laughed at my lack of adventure and walked up to the tattoo artist. She explained that she was in town for a visit and wanted something representative of the city. She left the creation of the idea up to him, and a half hour later she walked out with a beautiful tattoo of the word "jazz" imposed over a musical G clef. She loved it.

Could it possibly work between us? Was I changing from the unhappy, angry person to a more relaxed and happy woman? Had I discovered, examined, and changed enough of those behaviors that had pushed us apart? I believed that I had, and told Kat that I was willing to try to work things out if she felt the same way. I was so scared—my heart had been so broken, and here I was opening myself up again. What if it didn't work? But again, my mantra kept coming back to me—*I am not going to let my fears keep me from taking a leap of faith.*

We parted that morning, she to return to Louisville, me to continue on my adventure, but both of us filled with the hope of a new improved future together.

CHAPTER 11
What Might Have Been

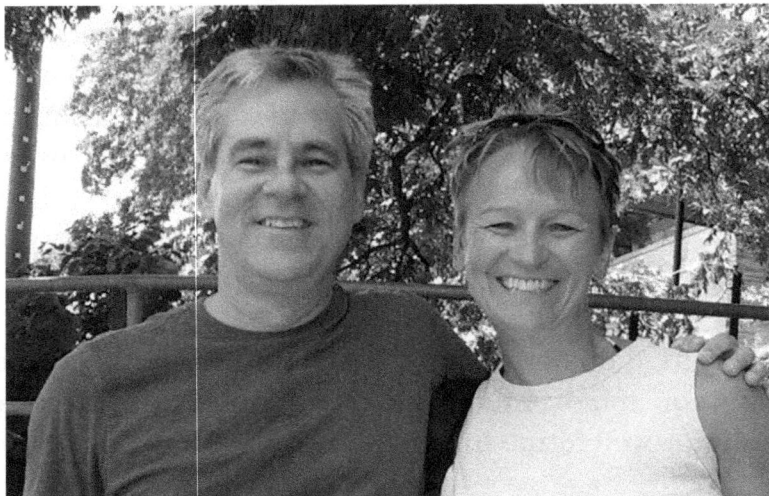

Leaving Kat and NOLA behind, I got in my trusty car and started the long drive west towards Texas. The summer had proved to be extremely hot, and I was grateful to be driving with the sun behind me. I drove through the swampy terrain of western Louisiana, and as the roads became flatter and the sky appeared larger, I finally entered the country's second largest state.

I carefully navigated through Houston at the height of rush hour in a short but intense thunderstorm, and after an hour turned north to make the final push on the back roads of State

Route 71 towards Austin and my friend Pat, another colleague from my University of Iowa days. Thankfully the rest of the drive was quite beautiful. There were green rolling hills and trees, and I passed ranch after ranch with herds of long-horned brown steers.

Pat had started his doctoral program about a year or so after I'd started mine. He was one of the strongest horn players I'd ever met, with the complete package: a consistent high and low range, technique, tone, and musicality. He was a quiet, mild-mannered man and seemed to have a calm demeanor no matter what the circumstances surrounding him. Likewise, when he played his horn, the appearance of his body and face stayed the same, whether he was playing high or low, loud or soft, fast or slow. So consistent and unchanged. In personality and horn-wise, he seemed to be the antithesis of me!

Pat and I shared a teaching assistant's office at Iowa, and early one afternoon in the middle of the week, Pat walked in and grabbed his horn. I was shocked to see him since I knew he had a recital that evening. Whenever I gave a recital, I always made sure to schedule it on a weekend. Two days before my recital, I'd do my heaviest playing; then the day before I'd do very little to no playing whatsoever, and hole myself up like a hermit to "rest my lip."

When I saw Pat early that day, I asked him, "What in the world are you doing here? You have a recital tonight!" In Pat's very quiet way, he replied nonchalantly, "Well, I have a quintet rehearsal," to which I replied with horror, "OMG, you have a recital tonight, and you're here at school for a rehearsal?!"

Pat laughed at me, explaining, "It's just like any other day."

We laugh about that to this day, but our own individual approaches worked well for both of us at the time. In retrospect, had I been more aware, I could have learned a valuable lesson from his "casual" approach, as my own rigid and regimented approach put so many conditions on my playing: recitals only on the weekend, I had to have the entire day off, my lips had to be rested to a certain degree, etc. Perhaps that could have been part of what contributed to my struggles and contributed to his continued success.

The year that the Mahler 3 Symphony was announced, our horn professor held auditions for the seating placement. Pat originally won the principal position; but a short time after the auditions, he was contacted by Ithaca College to fill in as professor of horn for the semester. He accepted the position and left. Subsequently I moved up to the principal spot and had the successful performance later on.

After the appointment at Ithaca, Pat moved on to a permanent position at the University of New Mexico for years before moving on to the University of Texas in Austin, which was why I was visiting him in Austin.

* * *

I arrived in Austin a bit after 7:30 and parked in front of Pat's apartment within a nice gated complex. Not five minutes later he drove up, and I tightly hugged yet another one of my University of Iowa horn colleagues. Pat gave me a tour of his apartment and introduced me to his handsome, sweet cat, Henry.

After the seven-hour drive I was looking forward to a cold beverage, so I stashed my bags, and we headed off in search of a decent beer. Pat pulled up in front of a local pizza and beer place called The Pour House, and we took a seat in the spacious patio area. I was thrilled to see an excellent selection of beer and accepted the server's recommendation of the pecan stout. We ordered a delicious pizza pie and enjoyed the warm, breezy evening as we caught up on each other's lives.

The next morning Pat headed off for an appointment while I caught up on blogging. On his way out the door, he asked me to listen to some horn ensemble pieces that he had composed.

I shook my head in wonder as I listened to the delightful music. I had always been in awe of him. Not only was he a phenomenal horn player and teacher, he was an excellent music theorist and also a really fine composer as these works attested. And to top it all off, just really down to earth and humble about his talents.

After he returned, we headed out for our day. We picked up his daughters, 14-year-old Sophie and 12-year-old Elsa. On top of being beautiful, smart, and sociable, they were also brass players, trumpet and French horn, respectively. We piled into the car and headed off for a short trip to Barton Springs Pool.

Barton Springs, a man-made recreational swimming pool in Zilker Park, maintains a year-round temperature of about 70 degrees. When we arrived, I was shocked to see that it was almost identical to Centennial Beach in Naperville, a similar type of quarry, where I'd spent most of every summer of my childhood.

Without hesitation, Pat jumped right in the cold, clear water. I gingerly walked down the stone stairs into about waist-deep water. Despite the 100-degree heat I couldn't take the cold water and retreated to dry land where the girls had perched themselves. Pat continued to splash around in the cold water, and I finally challenged myself to take the plunge. It was the coldest water I'd ever been in!

After dropping the girls off back home, Pat took me to the university and showed me around the music building, eerily quiet on the hot summer day. After a quick bite to eat, we drove off in search of a drink to top off the evening and found ourselves at Contigo, a fantastic out-of-the way open-air bar and restaurant. We sampled a local dark brew and enjoyed sharing tales of our musical exploits.

Being around Pat, seeing his success in his career, and talking about the old days made me yearn for the ability to play my horn as I had in the past. I couldn't help but have some regret that my life's path had taken me away from the life that I "should" have had. After receiving my doctorate, I was hired at the University of Louisville as the assistant professor of horn.

My dream of teaching at the college level had come true. But the pressure I continued to put on myself to conceal my playing problems and perform to a certain standard—now in a full-time professional job situation—brought about a decline in confidence and along with that, a rapid decline in my performance.

After my short two-year stint at U of L, I was not rehired. I gradually stopped applying for other teaching jobs, and I played and taught less and less as each year passed. At my lowest point, in utter despair that I'd lost my ability to play and, therefore, have a career as a college professor, I cried out to God, "Why would you take away the only thing that ever made me feel good about myself?" Like a thunderbolt, the answer immediately came hurtling back at me: "Because that's the only thing that makes you feel good about yourself."

I'd depended on my playing as the sole source of my self-esteem, and perhaps the lesson I needed to learn was that I was worthy just as Alise, and not as Alise the horn player. Maybe losing my ability to play was the only way I would ever figure that out.

I have learned that sometimes things happen in our lives that we think are the worst thing that could ever take place, but in retrospect they turn out to be the best thing to have happened. Kat and my breaking up was devastating for me. It seemed like the worst thing ever. However, I know for certain that had we not broken up, I wouldn't have had the catalyst to challenge my comfort zone; thus, I never would have set out on my Amazing Adventure.

CHAPTER 12
A Climb to Victory

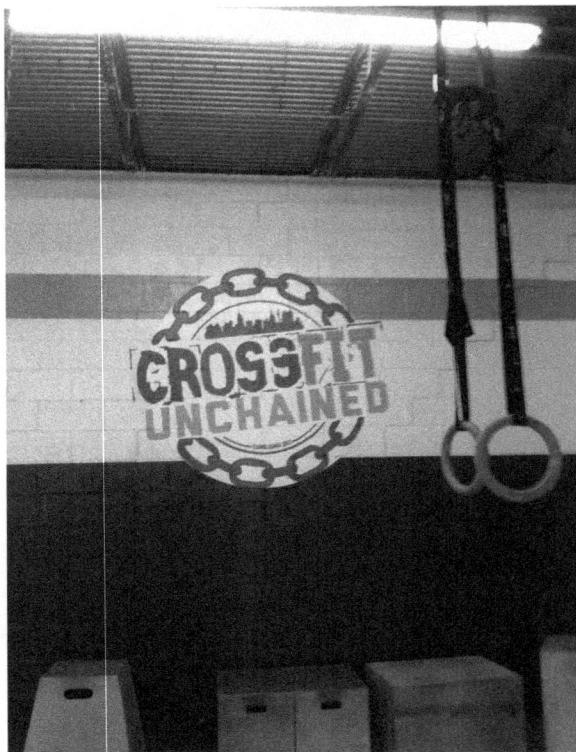

I was looking forward to my visit to San Antonio for two reasons: the history of the city and the fact that it would be only a short hour-and-a-half drive from Austin.

I left Austin around 9:30 a.m. and arrived in San Antonio a short time later, well before I could check into my hotel. With the whole day ahead of me, I followed the signs to downtown, parked my car, and headed towards the universal San Antonio recommendation: the Riverwalk. I spent about an hour walking up and down the length of the Riverwalk, looking into the shops and watching the river boat tours as they traveled down the river.

I still had plenty of time left in the day, so I headed north to the Alamo. When I finally saw it, I smiled as I remembered how everyone told me it was oddly placed in the middle of hotels and shops. Nonetheless, I got chills when I finally saw it in person. I stepped into the admission line, which was not very long, and soon was inside the walls of the historic building. I walked through the cool, dark interior and reverently observed the thick stone walls and the old artifacts of that famous battle so long ago—the rifles, knives, and other items. I finished inside that building and then walked around the grounds behind, entering the long stone barracks where I saw even more artifacts and read the history of the Alamo Mission and the independence of Texas.

After a rather late lunch I finally checked into my hotel, changed my clothes, and headed off to my first CrossFit visit in over a week. CrossFit Unchained was a short three-mile drive from the hotel, located adjacent to the I-35 overpass on East Houston Street. I walked in and introduced myself to Arthur, the owner, and he welcomed me to the gym and pointed me in the direction of the foam rollers. As I rolled out, I looked over at the whiteboard, on which the WOD (workout of the day) was written. Today's was going to be a 20-minute AMRAP (as many rounds as possible) of 1 rope climb, 10 sledge strikes on a tire, and a 25-meter sled/prowler push. When I saw the rope climb element of the class, I smiled and thought to a few years back.

I went to a Catholic school, Saints Peter and Paul, for grades 1 to 8. I was successful academically and musically, but not at all athletically. In junior high I was physically awkward as the onset of puberty had put uncomfortable unwanted pounds onto my previously little frame. Gym class was always intimidating for me. I felt so uncomfortable and out of place compared to everyone else (it seemed) who could run, jump, tumble, and climb with strength and ease.

One of the most daunting gym activities was the dreaded rope climb. I would watch other girls and boys grab the rope and, using their arms, legs, and feet, scamper effortlessly to the top of the rope and back down again. When my turn came, I'd stand on the padded blue mat, grab hold of the thick white rope, and try in vain to pull my heavy, cumbersome body up while the cool athletic kids snickered at my ineptness. I felt humiliated and a failure every time I saw that stupid rope.

One year into DCCF, I went in on a Saturday morning, which was unusual for me. Sean was running the session. I adored Sean. He was always smiling, always positive and encouraging, and treated everyone in the gym the same, regardless of their abilities. He announced that there would be no specific WOD that morning; rather, we were going to have a casual play-day learning some new skills, including Atlas Stone lifting, handstand pushups, and . . . rope climbs!

Immediately, I felt the pit of my stomach drop, and memories of my inept attempts at climbing a rope came flooding back. I walked up to Sean and the rope with increasing dread, confessing, "I've never been able to climb a rope."

I waited for Sean to turn into my old gym teachers and yell impatiently, "You just climb up!" But to my relief, Sean looked down at me gently and explained, "Oh! OK, here's how you do it."

Sean showed me how to loop the rope around one ankle and foot, and to use the rope and that one foot as a brace in order to "step" up a few feet with my legs, which then perfectly positioned me to grab higher onto the rope and climb up. Slowly and carefully, and with Sean's patient coaching, I pulled myself all the way up to the top of the 25-foot high ceiling. I paused at the top, peered down at Sean and my friends, who were all looking up at me with big smiles, and suddenly tears welled up in my eyes. That awkward, fat junior high Alise had just been vanquished.

I had to make a concerted effort to take control of my emotions in order to concentrate on Sean's instructions to descend the rope without a terrible rope burn. Once at the bottom, I allowed my tears to run unchecked, feeling like I had just unloaded a huge weight from my childhood.

* * *

The morning class at CrossFit Unchained was led by Coach Alisia, Arthur's wife. She was a beautiful, lithe, strong girl with a big smile and even bigger energy. The class was great fun— Alisia expertly taught us two different rope-climbing techniques. She was a patient and encouraging coach, just as Sean had been that morning at DCCF years ago. It was nice to try out a different technique than the one Sean had taught me, and I was proud of myself for being able to get up and down the rope throughout the entire 20-minute WOD (although I did get a pretty bad rope burn on the inside of my leg).

I've slowly realized why CrossFit became so meaningful to me. Throughout the years at DCCF, and so far in my drop-in visits in CrossFit boxes in Maryland, Florida, and Texas, I was accepted immediately into the community without question. Looking back at my awkward junior high years (and high school, for that matter), I felt like an outsider and just not good enough. Being part of CrossFit made me feel like one of the "cool kids," like part of a team.

CHAPTER 13
Red Rock and My Friend Red

As I shared earlier, when I first entertained the thought of an adventure, I emailed my dear friend Tonya, a stunning, porcelain-skinned redhead, vivacious and free-spirited. We'd known each other for years back in Louisville. Three years previously, she'd done the exact thing I'd only been contemplating—quit her job, sold her stuff, drove cross-country, and found herself in Sedona, Arizona. She'd been there ever since. I knew that she would relate to what was going on in my life and the reasons behind the desire to leave everything behind and find my true self.

After leaving Houston, I began the long, two-day trip to Sedona. I headed west on Interstate 20 through one of the most barren areas of Texas. With oil refineries spewing smelly smoke into the air, it was an especially bleak, ugly, and stinky drive. After finally merging onto Interstate 10, I ended up in the charming, tiny town of Van Horn, about 120 miles east of El Paso, offering a stunning view of the nearby Guadeloupe Mountains.

The next morning, once I left, immediately the landscape changed. Numerous majestic mountains appeared as I drove past Fort Hancock, Texas. I continued on through El Paso, and shortly after I crossed into New Mexico and through my first border checkpoint.

At Las Cruces, I started the long stretch towards Tucson and Phoenix. As I drove through these two very crowded and flat cities, all I could think of was how beautiful Tonya promised that Sedona would be! I turned onto I-17 North in Phoenix and finally started seeing some fantastic scenery. The final segment of the drive on Route 179 into Sedona almost blew my mind, as the famous Sedona Red Rocks appeared before me. What a great reward for a long 13-hour drive.

Because I'd gone through two time zones, it was only 4 p.m. when I pulled into Tonya's driveway—right at the base of Thunder Mountain. She was sitting out on the front porch, and I leapt out of my car and grabbed her in a huge bear hug. She introduced me to her fiancé, Chris, his adorable 8-year-old son, Alexander, and her friendly dog, Linus.

Sedona is a wonderful little town, surrounded by the most stunning and unique red rock mountains imaginable. It is overwhelming to be in the midst of such incredible beauty. Tonya and Chris' front porch faced Chimney Rock, and the back porch of the house overlooked Thunder Mountain, Sugar Loaf Mountain, Coffee Pot Mountain, and Munds Mountain. The first hour or so I was speechless as I took in the majesty of the surroundings.

Chris' good friend, Steve, joined us for dinner, and afterwards, I proudly brought out my Amazing Adventure map for Steve and Chris to look over. Chris is a former Marine and experienced hiker and survivalist. Steve is also an experienced hiker and very knowledgeable about just about anything. They took a look at the rest of my proposed route and strongly suggested that I make some adjustments in order to get to Glacier National Park earlier in the summer before the weather started turning colder. I took their advice and rearranged the remainder of my journey.

That evening, I could barely wait until it got dark enough to see the stars. Around 9:30 we went out on the back deck, and although it was a bit cloudy, I saw the most brilliant display of stars, along with the bright Milky Way. I wish that pictures could do it justice.

Finally, the long drive and the adjustment in time zones caught up with me, and I fell into an exhausted sleep.

The following day, after a full morning wandering around the local farmers' market and the shops of Tlaquepaque, Tonya and I joined Chris and Alexander for a late lunch. The change in altitude and the previous day's long drive was quickly catching up with me, so after lunch I caught a half-hour catnap.

I woke feeling much refreshed, which was good since Chris and Steve were taking me on a hike that evening. I eagerly brought out my new hiking shoes and backpack, and waited for Steve to arrive. Hiking is one of my favorite activities, and I was eager to hike with these two seasoned guys. We drove the short distance to the entrance to Long Canyon Trail and headed out.

Steve led the way and I worked hard to keep up with his long strides as Chris took up the rear. About a quarter of the way through Chris remarked that most folks he takes out start huffing and puffing at this point. I gave props to my conditioning and thanked him for the compliment.

Further along the trail, we hiked through some really rough and rocky terrain. At one point, we approached some shear rock and came up to a ledge. Chris effortlessly pulled himself up onto it. I looked at it and in my mind immediately thought, "I can't do that." My critical inner voice started to berate me. I had earned some respect so far on the hike, but now I was gonna blow it. How in the world was I going to get up that ledge? Were the guys going to have to boost me up? Would my failure to scale the ledge make us turn back because I couldn't handle it? I didn't say anything aloud, but my apprehension must have shown on my face.

Chris jumped back down and stood right next to me. "You can do this. Keep your hips close to the rock."

I did as he said, then found some footholds and slowly inched my way up. Chris' patient voice urged me on, "Good, keep going. Keep your hips forward, and you won't fall backwards."

I concentrated on his voice and the rock in front of me. Then, thanks to my strength, I was able to successfully pull myself up onto of the ledge. I had done it! It was further confirmation that we can always do more than we think we can.

I thought back to my coaching days at DCCF and the Y, and how many times class members faced a daunting task and did not believe they could do it. With good coaching and motivation, in most cases they'd been successful, and totally surprised themselves. Sometimes it takes someone else showing that they believe in us for us to believe in ourselves. In this instance, Chris did that for me.

Once we passed that spot, we came upon some incredible Indian ruins amidst the red rocks. To discover these isolated areas that most people don't see was an overwhelming experience, and I felt so lucky to have seen it.

On our return trip down the trail I followed Chris, who was in the lead. As we descended, I noticed that his step was effortless, like a mountain goat, for heaven's sake, and he moved down the trail with an ease of footing that I envied. On the other hand, I awkwardly hiked down the rocky trail, I stared at each footstep, and I could feel my brain working, "Which step is best? The rocks are loose there, I should avoid that step. Oops, watch out for that tree root, watch out for the uneven ground."

I realized that the more I thought about my footing, the more awkward and cumbersome it became. I looked at Chris' step, so effortless, and thought to myself, "I'm not going to think about it. I'm just going to let my footsteps fall where they want naturally." And lo and behold—my feet seemed to effortlessly find the right footing.

Our hike had started late in the afternoon, and as we neared the end, darkness quickly approached. Chris had prepared for this possibility; he had some headlamps just in case it got too dark. But, he called back, "I think we'll make it without them," and we continued on.

The darkness was disconcerting to me, "How in the world am I going to keep my footing in the rapidly enveloping darkness?" But a little voice told me to trust my senses, to trust that my footing would find itself, and to trust that my body would naturally discern what was on the trail in front of me. As far-fetched as that might sound, it worked. I never lost my footing in the dark although the trail was far from smooth and flat.

Later that summer, when I was reading Cheryl Strayed's book *Wild*, an absolutely enthralling account of her hike along the Pacific Crest Trail, I realized that I wasn't alone in recognizing the magical-like power that comes from having faith in your step. In *Wild* Strayed described an incident in which she was kicked out of a campground in the middle of the night and had to pack up her stuff and hike in total darkness. Her other senses took over, and she felt the trail and her body more acutely by just letting go and trusting her body and intuition to carry her safely along the trail. I knew exactly what she meant, for that's what I'd experienced in this night hike. I realized it was something big that I could apply to my whole view on life: let go and trust my step.

* * *

Sunday I woke late and made myself some coffee. After several quiet hours blogging on the front porch in the cool, late-morning breeze, I stretched and prepared for one last hike. From Tonya's front porch I'd been looking out at Chimney Rock for the past few days, and that's where I headed. All I had to do was walk out her front door and up the street about 100 yards, and I was at the base of the trail.

I turned left onto the Thunder Mountain Trail and started walking. Soon I came upon a rugged path on the right that headed up towards Chimney Rock. After about ten minutes I got intimidated because of all the scaling of heights this hike would involve. In case it's not apparent, let me say it directly: I have an acute fear of heights. So, I turned around and headed back towards the main trail.

But, dammit, this whole trip was about not letting fear rule me and about getting out of my comfort zone. I thought about my dad and how it appeared he'd played it safe within the confines of his comfort zone his whole life. I thought about all my old "uncomfortable" comfort zones. I thought about relationships I'd been in that weren't working, but that I'd been reluctant to leave because I wanted someone to take care of me. I thought about how unhappy I'd been in my job but how I'd been too scared to leave the security of it. I didn't want to back down from my fears again, so I told myself to get back up there, and everything would be OK if I was just smart and used my common sense.

I steadily climbed the red rocks, looking for firm hand and footholds, avoiding the agave plants known as "cowboy killers." Eventually I got quite close to Chimney Rock and congratulated myself on challenging my fear of heights.

Next came the hard part—finding my way back down again. I told myself that if I got up, I could get back down again, as long as I took my time, kept my center of gravity low, and used my common sense. I lost my footing at a few spots, but I kept low, sliding down on my butt. After some hunting and pecking for the best way back down, eventually I found myself back on the Thunder Mountain Trail.

I discovered a little enclosed spot under a tree that looked like an outdoor sitting area. I took off my pack, ate a snack, drank some water, pulled out my journal, and sat enjoying the stillness. It was devoid of all human noise; all I could hear was the cooing of some doves, the bugs buzzing past my ears, and the sound of the wind blowing through the trees. I sat in that idyllic spot with my eyes closed, enjoying the solitude and silence.

After my rest, I started in the opposite direction down the Thunder Mountain Trail. I laughed out loud as I came upon a sign pointing up: "Chimney Pass." I'd gone the hard way up first! This path easily brought me up the back of Chimney Rock, and the closer I got, I could see that Chimney Rock is actually three separate rocks; hence its other name of "Three Fingers."

Satisfied with my hike, tired, and nearly out of water, I headed back down to the bottom of the trail and back to the house. My time in Sedona was just about at an end, and I couldn't have been more pleased with the visit: I'd discovered myself physically capable of doing more than I thought I could. I trusted my step and found that it led me to confidence, safety, and wonder. It was one thing to experience this hiking a challenging trail. Could it be possible that trusting my step would transfer to other areas of my life? Could I learn to stop forcing, stop trying to control, and trust that my intuition would guide me to a life that would fall into place without struggle?

I'd already taken a leap of faith earlier in the year and discovered a positive result. Now I was charged to trust myself enough to do this in more areas of my life.

CHAPTER 14
My Kind of Town?

I left Sedona very reluctantly. I was so much at ease there and could have easily stayed much longer. Tonya and Chris were lobbying for me to consider it as my new home. But Flagstaff beckoned, and I'd heard really wonderful things about it; the size, the climate, and the liberal culture. Could I be heading to my new home?

The drive between Sedona and Flagstaff, north on 89A, was stunning, narrow winding roads through lush forests of pine. At the highest elevation of the trip, I saw a little turnoff for a scenic view. Tonya had suggested that I stop there, and I pulled off and beheld the most spectacular view—as close as I could manage without getting dizzy from my fear of heights. This scenic turnoff offered a pleasant surprise; it was lined with several Native American booths selling crafts, jewelry, and gifts. I searched for the perfect memento and finally decided on a lovely little money clip etched with my spirit totem, the wolf.

I arrived in Flagstaff a little bit after 1 p.m. and after one look decided that I would be staying more than just the night. I found historic Route 66 and followed it into the little downtown area, parked my car, and started walking down San Francisco Avenue.

Quaint is the word that accurately describes this little area. After checking out several outdoor gear shops, I found one with a much-needed hiking hat. I enjoyed a delightful and hearty Blackbird Porter at a local spot, the Flagstaff Brewing Company, and after walking out the door I passed a little music store. I'd been waiting for an opportunity like that. I walked inside and found what I'd been searching for since leaving Bethesda: a shiny little harmonica. I had plenty of time on the rest of my trip to learn how to play the damned thing! I drove back along Route 66, checked into my hotel, added an extra night, and relaxed. After a short rest, I ventured out, had a bite to eat at Diablo Burgers, picked up a few sweet little cigars, and was back to the hotel at dusk.

To my surprise and delight the following morning, the sun was up over the horizon by 5:30 a.m. I dressed quickly and headed over to CrossFit Flagstaff, a mere two miles from where I was staying. I walked in for the class and was greeted, not by the resident CrossFit dog, but by the resident CrossFit cat, Clark. Clark pointed me in the direction of the coaches, Stephen and Rachel. I introduced myself, bought myself a CrossFit Flagstaff shirt, and joined the warm-up.

This was one of the biggest and nicest CrossFit gyms I'd visited on my trip. We warmed up on our own; then Coach Rachel led us through a short barbell complex. There was no strength element to the class, but we went directly into the workout of the day, named the River Styx. It was a 1,000-meter row followed by 21-15-9 kettle bell swings and burpees. After well over a week without a gym workout, it felt great to move my body that way again.

After class, I headed across the street to a little coffee shop and enjoyed a cup of strong dark brew. I looked up and in walked one of that morning's crew. We talked just a bit, and it turned out he was originally from Macomb, Illinois, right down the road from my undergrad school, Eastern Illinois University. A fellow Midwesterner!

I proceeded to grill him about living in Flagstaff. "So, what's the weather like here?" I asked.

"It's quite nice. Not humid like it is in the Midwest. Being at 7,000 feet, there isn't air-conditioning really. We use swamp coolers instead. And there's lots of snow in the winter if you like to ski."

"What's the political climate like?" was my next question.

He replied, "It's pretty liberal. The University of Northern Arizona makes Flagstaff kind of like a mini Madison, Wisconsin, if you know what I mean."

I laughed. "I know exactly what you mean! Thanks for all your help."

"You're welcome. Hope I see you around the CrossFit box sometime soon!"

* * *

After grabbing a quick shower at the hotel, with the whole day in front of me I contemplated what to do. Tonya had suggested the chairlift at the Arizona Snow Bowl, but unfortunately it only ran Friday through Sunday. However, there was a decent little climb very close to me: the Elden Lookout Trail, 2.5 miles one-way and about a 2,000-foot elevation to the top. It was cloudy, relatively cool, and perfect for the climb. I drove a few miles to the trailhead and started my ascent.

The climb was more difficult than I'd expected—steep, very rocky, and quite strenuous. For just a short moment, as I looked up at the daunting climb ahead of me, I thought I was in over my head, but I told myself to keep my head down and keep putting one foot in front of the other.

Sometimes when we look at the magnitude of a task in front of us, it seems untenable. I think too often in the past I'd look at something and think, "I can't do that," and give up without trying. Like the prospect of opening my own gym that I was too scared to do by myself. But by concentrating on that one step just in front of us, one small step at a time covers that span and eventually brings us to the end. This was how I summited Mt. Elden!

At the top of Mt. Elden I was rewarded with a stunning view of Flagstaff. I was grateful to my physical preparedness but even more proud of myself for not giving up when the going got tough. I mean, no one else would have known if I had just turned around at the beginning of the climb.

After a tough workout that morning and an even tougher climb up Mt. Elden, I was beat. I made my way back to the hotel, took a well-deserved shower, and returned to Flagstaff Brewing Company for a second round. I chose a wonderful Coconut Porter and reflected on my impression of Flagstaff. I loved the size, the quaint feel of the downtown area, the accessibility of hiking trails in the area, and the fantastic CrossFit gym. Feeling optimistic about my settling down someplace new, I went back to my motel, nestled into bed, and looked forward to the next adventure ahead of me.

CHAPTER 15

Solitary and Spectacular

While I visited Sedona, Chris suggested that I go to the North Rim of the Grand Canyon rather than the South Rim because it was less crowded and touristy, so that's what I decided to do.

I left Flagstaff at 4:30 a.m., just as the sun began to lighten the sky in beautiful hues of blue and pink. I started the four-hour drive to the North Rim on the now-familiar Route 89 North. Off to my left I could see the faint outline of Humphrey's

Peak in the distance; I'd heard great things about hiking it and hoped to someday soon.

My drive continued, solitary and quite desolate. It was almost eerie how deserted the road was. After a couple of hours, I drove through Bitter Springs and turned onto Alt 89. At that point, I began to see some welcome change in the landscape. As I drove towards Marble Canyon, I had to pull off and snap a few spectacular shots of rocks and buttes with layers of multi-colored rock.

At the Navajo Bridge, I crossed the Colorado River. I looked down as I traversed the river and gasped in amazement. It was so vast! I was finally getting close!

Immediately after crossing the Colorado River, the landscape changed to forests of pine and the temperature dropped into the 60s as I entered the Kaibab National Forest.

At the very small town of Jacobs Lake, I turned south onto 67, the Grand Canyon Highway, and drove the last 25 miles to the park. As I entered a clearing in the forest, I saw a coyote flash across the road in front of me, a gaggle of wild turkeys, and then herds of bison.

I arrived at the ranger entrance and was greeted by a delightful young lady who asked, "How are you doing?"

"Overwhelmed," I replied.

She smiled.

After chatting briefly about my summer plans, she suggested that I purchase an annual pass to all the national parks. She handed over several maps and sent me on the final 12-mile drive to the visitor center.

A few minutes later as I was pulling into the parking lot, I caught a glimpse of the Canyon on my left and gasped aloud. Spectacular! I parked my car and walked up to a ranger in the visitor center. I'd identified a trail to hike that day, the Uncle Jim Trail, and she smiled and said it was a great choice. The trail winds through the forest to a point overlooking the canyon. She directed me back down the road about a mile to the Kaibab Trailhead parking lot where I would find the starting point of the hike.

Before I departed, I entered the lodge itself, walked out the back door, and beheld the magnificence of the Grand Canyon for the first time. I just cannot put into words that first look at the majesty of this natural wonder.

With growing excitement, I loaded my backpack with water, lots of snacks, and other essentials. I drove to the Kaibab Trail lot, parked my car, put on my sturdy hiking shoes, and by 9:30 a.m. entered the Ken Patrick Trail that would eventually turn off to the Uncle Jim Trail Loop.

Three times I stepped aside for groups taking mule rides on the trail, but for the most part it was a solitary hike. I saw only 5 or 6 other hikers at the most in the entire three hours. I thought back to earlier in the spring, when friends would ask me if I was concerned about traveling and hiking alone. Shouldn't I take a class in self-defense? Shouldn't I bring a gun for safety? I felt no need; I trusted myself not to put myself in any position that would feel unsafe, but mostly, I felt that arming myself would put out fearful negative energy. I felt certain that if I put out loving trusting energy that it would be returned to me. So far, it had been working!

The trail was fairly flat and easily negotiated, aside for piles of mule poop. After two hours, I reached the far end of the loop, followed a very narrow path up small stone stairs, and came to the isolated point overlooking the canyon. It was dizzyingly gorgeous. Pictures don't adequately portray the vast scope of the canyon.

I sat as close to the edge as I was comfortable and munched a crisp apple as I enjoyed the silence all around me, save for the wind and the buzzing bees.

After a short rest, I got up, dusted myself off, and continued the loop back to the trailhead. The trail was so lightly traveled that once I got off the Uncle Jim Loop and back to the Ken Patrick Trail, I could see my footprints from the beginning of my hike.

When I finally cleared the trail back to the parking lot, I walked back up to the lodge and took the short half-mile Bright Angel Point Trail around the lodge. This little trail, with an incredible view of the Grand Canyon North Rim at the end, challenged my fear of heights. I got as close to Bright Angel Point as I could before finally turning back.

Even though the narrow path to the point had railings on both sides, I just could not overcome the feeling of terrifying vertigo the vast height induced. At times, it felt so scary that I wanted to crawl on my hands and knees. I looked out to the end of the path, where several tourists perched at the very end of the point. I envied them but enjoyed the magnificent view from where I stood safely—in my comfort zone.

CHAPTER 16

Facing My Fears

Z ion National Park was not originally a destination on my Amazing Adventure Map. But my Sedona friends said that if I planned to go to Bryce Canyon, I must also go to nearby Zion National Park. So, I picked Kanab, Utah, as my home base for the next couple of days, which was just a short drive to either park.

On a hot sunny morning, I headed northwest for the short 45-minute drive to Zion National Park. In passing through the admission gate, the entire landscape changed. The most breathtaking rock formations appeared before me, huge red sandstone, nothing like I'd seen the week before at the Grand Canyon. I was truly in amazement, barely crawling along at 10 to 15 miles per hour and stopping frequently to take pictures of the unbelievable views all around me. As I got close to the park itself, I drove down several switchbacks overlooking the canyon, getting close to the edge, with more unique and amazing rocks appearing in front of me.

At the visitor center I spoke with a ranger, admitting that I knew nothing about the park and was unfamiliar with any of the hikes, but that I was in great shape and was looking for a challenge. She suggested that I take the Angel's Landing Trail via the West Rim Trail. She recommended that I hike all the way up the West Rim Trail, through the switchbacks at Walters Wiggles, and up to Scout's Lookout, which overlooks the canyon. She said that the last half-mile of the trail went up to Angel's Landing. It was a very strenuous climb, often very narrow with nothing on either side. She set me at ease, though, saying that if my fear of heights was too much, I could climb up to the lookout and turn around there.

Satisfied, I walked out, ready to go.

Zion had a fantastic shuttle bus system. I jumped on one of them and headed towards my stop. I got off the bus at the grotto, full of excitement, and walked over to the trailhead.

After an extremely solitary hike the week before at the Grand Canyon, I was surprised to see so many people. It also surprised me that the trail was paved, like a sidewalk. After hiking up rugged trails in Sedona, Flagstaff, and the Grand

Canyon, it seemed a bit odd. After a while though, I was to be grateful for the footing it provided.

The hike started off pretty easy and offered a fantastic view of the Virgin River running through the canyon. I spotted several deer along the banks of the river and relished the scenery as I climbed upwards.

Eventually, the path became steeper and the switchbacks more challenging. I also noticed how narrow the trail became and how close I was to the edge of the canyon the higher I got. The final switchbacks to Scout's Lookout were dizzyingly steep, and I remember thinking that this hike could rival any CrossFit workout. Breathing hard, I passed a woman on her way down who smiled at my sweaty face and said encouragingly, "Not much further!" I finally stepped out into the open and onto Scout's Lookout.

Scout's Lookout was a fairly flat, long rock at the top of the canyon. There were no guardrails or other protective devices surrounding the lookout. I sat down a safe distance from the edge, took off my backpack, and tentatively snapped some pictures as I ate a snack.

Directly to my right, I saw the infamous Angel's Landing. I was surprised to see scores of hikers scaling up and down the rock, despite the ranger's description of the difficulty of the climb. It looked quite daunting, with a rope chain up the side and a huge sign warning of the risk and danger of the hike. I watched little 8-year-old kids coming and going. I watched people much older than I coming and going. Big, small, tall, short, young, old—going up and coming down with sweaty, triumphant smiles on their faces. I knew that the longer I sat and stared at it, the more scared I would get. Finally, after seeing a man in his late 60s coming down, I thought if he could do it, I could do it.

I walked over to the base and stared . . . and stared and stared. I just could not get myself to take that first step. The warning signs, those chains, my experience with the edges of the Grand Canyon, and my earlier hike up and looking out on Scout's Lookout, my all-encompassing fear of heights—all of that overwhelmed me, and I walked back to the safety of the lookout.

I sat there for a half hour and chided myself over and over, "Alise, you're in fantastic shape, you're a badass, you crossfit for God's sake. Imagine Erin's voice encouraging you and motivating you, this trip is all about facing all your fears and conquering them, c'mon, just fucking do it!"

I couldn't.

Defeated and deflated, I turned around and walked the long way back down to the bottom of the trail, tears streaming down my face. I tried to hide my sobs from the hikers heading up the trail. I felt like a failure. I felt that the fact that I could not bring myself to hike that final half-mile up to the top of Angel's Landing that somehow that made me inadequate. Twice as I was heading down I stopped and thought about going back up to try it . . . but didn't.

I drove back to my motel room, and once inside, I cried my heart out. I tried to understand why it affected me so much. Why was I so hard on myself and why did I feel that I'd failed? If anyone else had told me they had the exact experience, I would have wrapped my arms around them and compassionately counseled them to be easy on themselves, to look at what they had achieved—a very successful and challenging hike in one of the most beautiful parks in the world. Why did I feel that I didn't deserve the same compassion from myself?

I felt that deep down, for whatever reason, I was inadequate and just not good enough. Instead of looking at the wonderful things I had been doing the past several weeks, months, or even my whole life for that matter, I looked at that one small thing and used it as confirmation of my unworthiness. "See, Alise, you couldn't climb Angels Landing, you couldn't conquer that fear of heights, so that proves that you aren't good enough."

What I didn't realize then was that it was my ego talking. That insidious critical voice in my head had me convinced that it was the voice of reason, that it knew best, and that it was only hard on me to make me stronger. That voice had been telling me my entire life that I was lazy, that I wasn't smart enough, and that I was just not good enough. It had made me so afraid of failure that I had an excuse to never try to do anything. But, I began to realize that any voice inside of me that spoke so negatively could not be my true, authentic, loving self.

Although that ego voice had been whispering in my ear for my whole life, at that moment when I recognized it, I started to slowly let go of its hold over me.

One day I hope to return to Angels Landing, approach it without fear, and make the climb to the top. But, if I get there and that doesn't happen, I will tip my hat to the mountain and proudly walk away.

CHAPTER 17

A HooDoo of a Lesson

The next day, I contemplated skipping Bryce Canyon and going back to Zion to face Angels Landing again. But, I decided to just let it go.

I packed up all my stuff, said goodbye to the pretty town of Kanab, and drove the hour and a half trip to Bryce Canyon. The landscape was fairly non-descript, but suddenly when I entered the Dixie National Forest and Red Canyon, I was astounded. I followed a few short miles of incredible red sandstone formations, including little tunnels built into the rock. What a pleasure! And then, in a blink of an eye, I drove out of it.

Once I arrived at the park, I found the visitor station. The ranger on duty suggested I take the most popular hike, the Queens Garden/Navajo Loop. I asked if there was something a bit longer, and he suggested that I take the Peekaboo Loop to extend the hike. Prepared with my maps, I drove to Sunrise Point right next to Bryce Lodge and parked my car.

I had a little trouble initially finding the trailhead and felt just the tiniest tinge of frustration. I asked directions from a couple walking toward me. She pointed behind the lodge, explaining, "Once you see the rim, everything will make sense."

I walked down a path and beheld my first spectacular view of Bryce Canyon, a canyon of the most spectacular-looking rock called Hoodoos. The Hoodoos were like sandcastles kids make by taking wet, wet sand and dripping it through their hands.

I followed the trail, joining throngs of people walking down into the canyon. I heard families speaking French, German, and Chinese. Deeper into the canyon I walked, sometimes very close to a steep drop-off.

At the bottom of the Queens Garden Trail I turned left onto the Navajo Loop and followed the path into a woodsy area at the very bottom. I arrived at Peekaboo Pass, but it appeared to me that a sign indicated that the section was closed. I watched for a while but didn't see anyone else take that path. I was confused and a bit exasperated. I wanted to take that loop, and I wondered why the ranger had suggested it if it was closed. Disappointed, I continued back up the Navajo Loop.

I finally came out at Sunset Point and saw another ranger there. I asked about the Peekaboo Loop and she said it was indeed open, but the connector to Bryce Point a ways down the loop was closed due to a landslide.

Goddammit! For the first time on my trip, a flood of irritation overcame me, and I almost snapped at the ranger impulsively until I caught myself—this wasn't her fault. I heard my inner judge begin the lecture: whoever was in charge should have made that signage on the Peekaboo Pass clearer. My irritation with the park increased as the little voice spoke louder. I had my hike all planned out, and now it was spoiled. It was only 10:30, and I didn't want to backtrack to my starting point.

Suddenly, it hit me that this was the first time on my trip that I'd felt angry or irritated. My plan hadn't gone the way I wanted, and I recognized that I was falling back into my pattern of being upset when my comfort zone was breached and threatened. I took a deep breath and let it out. That was the old angry, controlling Alise, and I wanted no part of that on my adventure.

I had spent tons of energy in the past in angst when things didn't go my way or the way I thought they *should*. I would replay the offense over and over in my mind, becoming more distressed and angry or unhappy. I wasted so much energy that I missed the present moment.

I was grateful for being mindful enough to recognize that, and I made a choice. I told myself to let it go and to enjoy the moment. It was a gorgeous day, I was in a stunning national park, and I was on a trip of a lifetime. There was NOTHING to be unhappy about. I walked back up to the lodge to a waiting shuttle bus. I decided to take the shuttle and see the two points that I would have seen had I taken the extra trail. I climbed onto the bus and headed to Bryce Point. The bus driver explained that it was possible to walk along the rim from Bryce Point all the way back to Sunrise Point, where' I'd started that morning. I decided to take his advice.

I began walking along Bryce Point, continued down to Inspiration Point (very exposed, sheer, and scary), all the way down to Sunset and then arrived at Sunrise Point. Altogether I had about a four-hour hike, and I actually saw more of the canyon than I would have with my original plan.

I smiled to myself as I realized the Universe had presented me with a lesson. Sometimes our plans don't go the way we expect them to. Sometimes things happen that are out of our control. Rather than dwell on that over which you have no control, have faith that perhaps something better is yet to come. As I found out that day, sometimes the unexpected is a welcome surprise!

CHAPTER 18

A Coincidental Visit

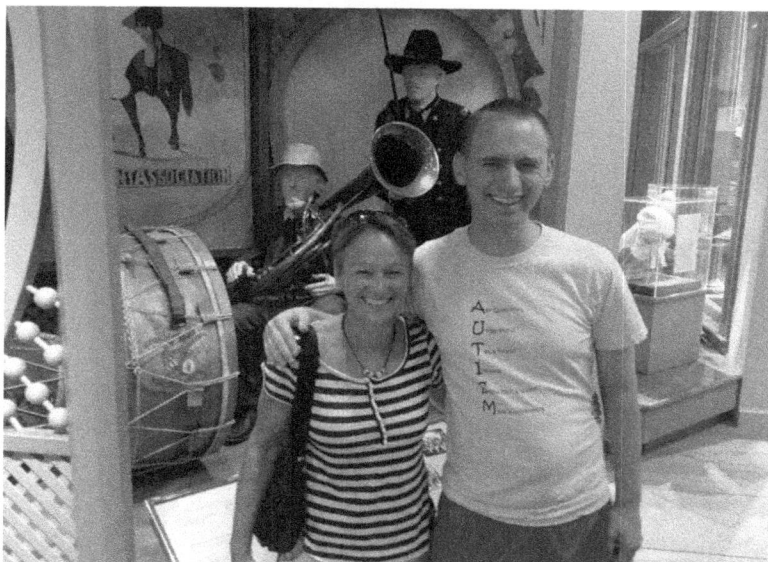

A fter my adventures in Sedona, Flagstaff, the Grand Canyon, Zion, and Bryce, I was exhausted. I wanted some time to rest and recharge my batteries. I was also getting a bit lonely, which surprised me since I thought I was so comfortable being alone. But it had been over a week and a half since I'd left Tonya and Chris, and before that I'd been visiting other friends at pretty frequent intervals. I had seen such incredible sights and scenery, and had hiked mountains and canyons, and although it was wonderful, those experiences almost seemed less special without someone to share them with.

I booked myself a room in beautiful Salt Lake City for a couple of days and posted on Facebook that I was headed that way. Immediately, I received a response from my former horn student Cameron, who said he, his mom, and sister would be in Salt Lake City the next day, would I still be there? I jumped at the chance to see old friends, and we made a plan to connect.

* * *

I'd met Cameron several years earlier when he was a freshman at Jeffersonville High School. My dear friend Scott Cooksey, the band director at the high school, had asked if I'd be willing to take Cameron as a student. "Of course!" I replied. Scott continued, telling me that Cameron had Asperger's, a mild form of autism. "Makes no difference to me!" I replied. I was happy to teach any and all of Scott's horn players.

Later that evening I learned a bit more about Asperger's as I'd not had any experience with any students on the spectrum. I discovered some social interaction and communication characteristics for me to be aware of. After that, I spoke to Cameron's mother, Jen, and we set up a lesson for one Saturday morning.

That morning, in walked Cam, a tall, thin, gangly young man. After the lesson, I distinctly remember thinking he appeared no different than any other 14-year-old boy I'd met! From that day on, I developed the most wonderful friendship with Cameron. He possessed an incredible enthusiasm, joy, and passion for the horn. He was a diligent student and made great strides from that first lesson through his senior year. Even more importantly, he was a kind, compassionate, and friendly young man who found a home in the Jeffersonville

High School Band and was well loved by all of them. He was one of my favorite students ever, and I am so proud of him and all he accomplished.

After high school, Cameron spent a couple of years on a mission trip in North Carolina. Then he enrolled as a music major at Brigham Young University Idaho. He had just completed his first semester there, and his mom and sister were picking him up and bringing him back home until January. Salt Lake City was on their way home.

I contacted Jen and told her where I was staying and asked where we should meet up. "Temple Square!" she said. "It will be easy to find." I drove up I-15 and sure enough, I couldn't miss it. I walked in the south entrance to the square and was about to text Jen when I saw Cameron walking toward me.

Still the same old Cameron after all these years, but he was losing his boyish features and turning into a man. We hugged and walked over to his mom Jen and sister Jamie. Jamie had just had her wisdom teeth extracted and wasn't feeling well, so Jen sent me and Cameron to tour Temple Square while she attended to Jamie.

First, we went into the Tabernacle, the original home of the Mormon Tabernacle Choir. I was thrilled to see it and longed to hear them sing in there. And to hear the magnificent organ, constructed with over 11,000 pipes. At that moment, two girls were up front giving an acoustical demonstration of the Tabernacle. First, one of them tore a sheet of paper in thirds, and I could clearly hear that all the way in the back where we were seated. Next, I saw her drop three things into a bowl, and by the sound I assumed they were little rocks. But Cameron told me no, those were pins dropping! It's true, the acoustics in the Tabernacle are such that you really can hear a pin drop.

Next, Cameron brought me to the Assembly Hall, a lovely, more intimate building with beautiful stained-glass windows and a smaller although still-impressive organ. Finally, we walked across the street to the conference center. We were greeted by a young man who invited us to take a tour of the building. A small group of us spent nearly 45 minutes walking through the center. Not only is the conference center a huge, 20,000-seat hall where the Mormon Tabernacle Choir currently performs, but it also housed some incredibly beautiful works of art—painting, sculptures, glassworks, and the most beautiful gardens on the roof of the building.

After finishing our tour, we met up with Jen and Jamie at the History Museum, where Jen snapped a picture of us in front of a display of old instruments. We all hugged as we said our goodbyes.

I told them how grateful I was to have had the chance to meet up with them. It was almost as if the Universe had heard how lonely I was and arranged for that chance meeting. Coincidence or not, as Dr. Wayne Dyer states, I was comforted to see some friends from back home.

CHAPTER 19

Too Much For One Day

A fter a couple of restful days in Salt Lake City, I headed north to Grand Teton National Forest.

The drive from Idaho Falls to Grand Teton National Park was one of the most beautiful drives of the summer. I took the Swan Valley Highway, and not far after I started I stopped at a little scenic view for a spectacular shot of the gorgeous Snake River.

I came over a ridge and then drove down into the town of Swan Valley. It was impressive to look down into the valley and see the Snake River winding through the town. Once in town, I made a left and headed north through some farmland but still among the mountains.

I entered the Targhee National Forest, surrounded by tall, statuesque, and fragrant pines. The road wound higher and higher. Finally, I arrived at the town of Victor and crossed into Wyoming. I encountered a scary but breathtaking drive through Teton Pass with an incredibly steep 10% grade. I was a bit unnerved to notice my brakes feeling bumpy and a bit insecure, so I drove with extra caution. Suddenly I looked to my left, and there were the Tetons, covered with snow! Finally I turned into Teton Village and then into the park.

I found the visitor center and talked to a nice young ranger. He suggested that I stop at both Taggart Lake (there are moose around!) and Jenny Lake. I took my map and headed north. At the Taggart Lake Point, sure enough, I saw a throng of people to the right, and there back among the trees was a moose! I snapped a few shots, wishing my lens was better, and continued on.

I arrived at Jenny Lake around noon. I got out of my car, stretched, threw my backpack on, and walked about halfway around the beautiful lake. An hour or so later, I got back in my car and continued through the rest of the park, passing Jackson Lake and Jackson Dam.

After about a half hour driving north, I entered Yellowstone National Park at the south entrance at around 2:30 p.m. The drive through the Tetons had taken me much longer than I'd expected. I had hoped to drive the entire Yellowstone loop, but there was not enough time for that. I was exhausted from my early departure that morning, and I wished I could just stop for the day right there. But it would be impossible to get a room in Yellowstone then, and I'd already made a reservation for the night all the way in Bozeman, so I just had to keep pushing through.

I knew for certain I wanted to see Old Faithful, so I headed onto the western portion of the loop after touching base at the visitor center at Grant Village. As I drove towards Old Faithful, the skies darkened, and it looked ominously like rain.

I arrived at Old Faithful around 3:15 and found my way right up to its edge. A crowd was already surrounding the geyser, and I asked when it was next scheduled to erupt, and folks told me about 20 minutes. We sat there, and sure enough, right on schedule, there it went, a hot geyser of water shooting up into the breeze. I smiled and joined the crowd in applause.

* * *

Now it was getting late, and I still hadn't gotten all the way to the north entrance, so I quickly got in my car and drove on. I passed through Madison and Norris, stopping briefly for a cursory look at several hot springs and pools of hot, smelly, sulfurous, gassy water. I felt pangs of regret that I had to rush through and would miss so much of Yellowstone. At this point, I was just taking hurried pictures to enjoy later. At Norris I turned north, and finally arrived at Mammoth Hot Springs, where herds of moose relaxed right in the center of the little city square.

I drove out of the park and headed north towards Montana. I was exhausted and had learned my lesson—Teton and Yellowstone in one day was too much. But the bigger lesson I learned was that I still had to learn to relax and be present in the moment. I had gotten carried away, as I had often in my past, in planning and cramming too much in for one day, and not giving myself any wiggle room whatsoever. The price I paid was not being able to fully enjoy either park.

I remembered earlier in the trip saying to my friends and family that I was just going to take my time, be spontaneous, take the back roads, and stop whenever something caught my eye. I guess it was good that this happened and that I recognized what I had done. And now I had a good reason to return to Yellowstone in the future and pick up where I'd left off.

CHAPTER 20

The Immensity of the Sky

Montana—the state I'd been dreaming about since I first contemplated the journey. This state had fascinated me ever since I watched *A River Runs Through It*. All I had been able to think about was how much I wanted to see the immensity of the sky in this state.

After I left Teton and Yellowstone National Parks, I headed that way. As I entered the state, the Absaroka and Gallatin Mountains immediately appeared before me—gigantic, overwhelming, and just a bit ominous. Perhaps it was because of the dark, cloudy sky, but I felt intimidated, small, and scared as I drove through them.

Then I noticed the beautiful Yellowstone River right next to me. It wound around and beside the interstate, back and forth, sparkling and crystal clear, brightening my spirits as I drove along the lonely road.

Finally, I drove over the crest of a hill, and the city of Bozeman appeared before me, surrounded by more majestic mountains. I took my exit and, shortly after, pulled into the parking lot of my home for the night, The Rainbow Motel. As soon as I saw it, my heart dropped. From the outside, it appeared shabby and dated, something I would have stayed at years ago when I was traveling with my family as a kid.

"Well," I thought, "it's only for one night."

I walked into the tiny lobby, and a sturdy, no-nonsense but friendly Montana-bred woman checked me in. I chuckled as she handed over my room key, it was a plastic old-fashioned key. With some trepidation at the door of my room, I opened the door and walked in—to one of the cleanest, most well-maintained rooms that I'd been in on my entire trip. The bedding was brand-new and inviting. The towels were snow white and soft. The bathroom was spotless. I was relieved and delighted.

Exhausted from a long day in two national parks and too tired to go out for food, I poured myself a bourbon, grabbed a little sweet cigar, and walked outside to enjoy the sun setting— at 9:45 p.m.! It was so beautiful and peaceful. I enjoyed the night breezes and the colors of the sky.

The next morning, I woke very hungry. I checked out of my hotel and headed downtown to a highly recommended little diner, The Western Cafe. I walked in and was instantly taken with it. This little spot was cozy and inviting, decorated like a page out of *Field and Stream*, with country music playing in the background. I took a seat at the counter and immediately a rugged bearded guy with an earring and tattoos brought me a mug of strong coffee and a menu. I ordered the biscuits and gravy with two eggs over easy. It appeared in no seconds flat. It was one of the best breakfasts I'd ever had.

While I was eating, a stocky middle-aged man with curly gray hair sat next to me at the counter. He was obviously a regular—everyone greeted him by name, Rick—and the bald guy at the counter brought him coffee and juice as soon as he sat down.

Rick turned to me and commented, "It's sure been hard to get around with all that construction downtown."

"I'm just passing through, so I haven't noticed," I explained.

He asked, "Where you from?"

"Kentucky."

"Well, I been living in Montana my whole life. What brought you to Bozeman?"

So, I told him what I'd been up to.

He was fascinated and called over the owner of the cafe, whom he introduced as Susan, telling her, "This young lady quit her job, sold her house, and is driving around on an adventure!"

Susan looked at me in amazement and exclaimed, "Honey, that takes a lot of guts!"

I sat there long after I'd finished eating, drinking coffee, and talking to these friendly folks. I had the best vibe in there. I could have stayed all day.

Finally, I paid my bill, and as I got up from the counter and said my goodbyes, Susan walked over with a bag of food for me, put her hand on my arm and said, "Here you go, hon, for the road."

I got a lump in my throat and was on the verge of tears, so touched by the kind and generous gesture by a perfect stranger.

I thanked her sincerely, and headed west with a happy heart. I was starting to experience that you get back what you put out.

I headed west on Interstate 90 towards Missoula. With a clear blue sky and the sun shining brightly, I finally saw what I'd only imagined in my mind—the immensity of the sky in Montana. It was so immense that I just couldn't capture it in the limited frame of a camera.

After an hour and a half of very flat terrain, the mountains appeared before me again, and I noticed another beautiful creek winding alongside me. It was so pristine and isolated and inviting, and I was determined to find a way to get right next to it. About twenty miles outside of Missoula, I noticed a little exit for a state park. I turned off the interstate and made my way to a tiny little campground/park called Rock Creek Recreation Area. I drove down a lonely little road, and there I saw it: Rock Creek, famous in Montana for excellent fishing.

I thought it was the most beautiful thing I'd ever seen. The water was crystal clear, and I could see every single rock in it. I looked downstream; the creek was lined with trees in full greenery, contrasting sharply with the deep blue of the sky. In the distance, I saw a lovely mountain. It was the image of Montana that I'd always imagined. I sat there for about a half hour enjoying the solitude and my own private perfect postcard view.

After a final half hour of driving, I arrived in Missoula and checked into my motel on the far west side of town, past the airport. I planned to be there at least two days. I needed to have my brakes looked at—they had worried me on Teton Pass—and I wanted to make sure they were serviced before I continued on my journey. I called a local brake shop and made an appointment for the following morning. I drove to the heart of the lovely Missoula downtown area and found a little local spot, Iron Horse Bar, where I ate a couple of delicious sliders and some sweet potato fries as I enjoyed a White Sox/Tigers game on TV.

The next morning, I loaded up my backpack with my computer and snacks, just in case my car required a long repair. I drove downtown and dropped it off, found a little local coffee spot, City Brew, enjoyed a cup of strong coffee, and caught up on my blog. Feeling hungry, I wandered several blocks before I stopped in yet another local spot, The Hob Nob, and enjoyed an amazing corned beef hash breakfast.

As I walked out the door I heard music. I popped my head back in the restaurant and asked if they knew where it was coming from. The girl at the register replied that Missoula holds a lunchtime concert series every Wednesday called Out to Lunch, down by the river at Caras Park, with food trucks, live music, and activities for kids. How lucky was I to be in town in order to enjoy that!

Excitedly I made my way across the Higgins Street Bridge that spanned the Clark Fork River. The sound of the river beckoned me. I made my way down to the rocky banks, took my shoes off, and stepped into the cold, clear, beautiful water and fulfilled another one of my dreams—to have my feet in a Montana river. I sat on a rock by the river and watched a uniquely Missoulian pastime: boogie boarders riding Brennan's Wave. I'm quite sure it was the first time I'd ever seen anyone surfing on a river!

The sun shone warmly on my shoulders as I looked around me. Missoula is in a valley and is completely surrounded by mountains. Every direction I looked, I could see them, some still capped with a faint hint of snow, even this late in the summer. Looking out into the big Montana sky, I felt that my soul was at peace. It was as if I really could feel the presence of God, in me, and all around me, emanating from the immensity of the sky.

I walked up the bank into Caras Park, enjoyed a little music coming from the stage, and walked through the long, tented pavilion with a variety of food vendors. I found a little ice cream stand, The Big Dipper, and asked the girl in the truck what she would recommend, and she said, "Well, you're in Montana, you have to try the huckleberry!" I opted for that and was contemplating a second scoop when she suggested the Mexican chocolate. It was delicious! I wandered around the park and then along the picturesque Riverwalk, reveling in the magnificence of the river, the lively music, and the smiling people enjoying the beautiful afternoon. I felt as if the Universe had just handed me the most wonderful gift.

My phone rang—my car was ready for me, and it was only 12:30! I walked the short distance to the shop and picked up my car, which had nice, new front rotors. I made my way back to my motel and wrote the remainder of the afternoon.

That evening, I sat outside on a picnic bench on the grounds of my motel and witnessed one of the most stunning sunsets I'd ever seen. It was the end of the most perfect day. I felt like I had found my home.

CHAPTER 21

The Elusive View at Flathead Lake

Flathead Lake was unknown to me until Kat sent me a message saying she'd seen a segment on this beautiful place on CBS Sunday Morning. In researching it I learned it is the largest natural freshwater lake west of the Mississippi. From looking at images of it, I couldn't wait to see it in person.

The picture in my head

I made a reservation the following night in Kalispell, which is north of Flathead Lake. I had two choices: to drive from south to north on one side of Flathead Lake (either 93 or 35) and only see half of it, or to drive all the way around and then back up again. Since I was starting so early that day, I decided to see the entire lake and then some.

I left Missoula early on a crisp cool summer morning and headed north on Route 93. Soon I beheld some beautiful mountains on my right. I stopped at a little informational pull-off and learned that they were the Mission Mountains.

Finally, I came to a scenic view pull-off, and there it was, in the distance—my first view of Flathead Lake, shimmering in the early morning sunlight.

I pulled into the little tourist town of Polson, Montana, at the southern tip of the lake. I decided to start driving up the lake on the eastern side, Route 35, starting my quest to find the view that I'd seen so many times on Google. I couldn't wait!

As I drove I noticed the road didn't offer good views of the lake. Not yet at least. The road was very narrow and windy, with no place at all to pull off. I did see many cherry stands, so I stopped and picked up two pounds for five dollars.

Continuing my drive, I found a little state park and pulled into that, hoping to get access to the lake. I walked down to the shore and looked out onto the lake. It was lovely, but I still hadn't found the elusive spot.

I made it to the town of Bigfork. I'd read about this town—it was supposed to have great views of Flathead Lake. But I couldn't seem to find any direct access to the lake.

I was now at the northern edge of Flathead Lake. Everything I'd read had indicated that the east side had the best views. But, it was early, and I had plenty of day left. I drove west on 82 until I reached 93 and turned south, hoping that the west side of the lake drive would bring me to the elusive view.

* * *

I saw another likely spot and pulled into the Lakeside Volunteer Park. I walked down to the edge of the water and stepped in. Oh, so cold and clear. It was refreshing on that warm sunny day.

By now I'd ended up back in the town of Polson again and headed back up the east side of the lake again, heading towards Kalispell and my motel for the night. I didn't think I missed a good view the first time around, but I kept looking. I had seen a perfect spot for lunch on the way up, so I stopped and had a delicious emu burger and a rich chocolatey brew. I finished lunch and headed north towards Kalispell, leaving Flathead Lake behind me.

I learned a lesson that day: sometimes we have a picture in our mind of what we are going to see or a story of how something is going to turn out, and often that doesn't happen. I never did see the spectacular images of Flathead Lake that I'd seen on my computer. Who knows what season it had been taken, the time of day, what kind of camera, from what angle—all those variables? But despite that, I had a wonderful time driving around the lake, and it is indeed unbelievably beautiful. (But it would have been nice to have caught that view!)

CHAPTER 22
You Get Back What You Give

I was on my way to Glacier National Park—the ultimate destination of my Amazing Adventure. I'd been looking forward to visiting this park since I circled the entire state of Montana on my map in mid-February. "You have to see Going-to-the-Sun Road if you go to Glacier" was the advice everyone gave me. I planned to drive the entire length, back and forth, in a day.

A few days before, I was online doing some research on the park and just happened to stumble (or did the Universe lead me?) onto a link for the Red Bus Tours of Glacier. It was the perfect way to experience the day. I wouldn't have to drive the narrow mountain roads, and since I wouldn't be driving, I'd be able to see everything. I could just sit back and relax. I made a reservation for the all-day tour that would take me the entire length of Going-to-the-Sun Road and back.

The morning of the big day I woke early, filled with excitement. It was quite cool, without a cloud in the sky. It would be a glorious day. I left Kalispell about 7:15 a.m. and headed north.

The sun was shining brightly almost the entire way, but as I approached Columbia Falls, an enormous pine-covered mountain appeared before me, so large that it blackened the sky as if dark clouds had fallen. I drove alongside the mountain, with the Flathead River sparkling on the other side of me. Deeper and deeper I drove into the pine-covered mountains. Finally, I arrived at the fee station and entered the park. As I passed through the gates, a beautiful brown doe bounded across the road. I looked to my left and following close behind her were two little white-spotted fawns. They disappeared so quickly I didn't have time to pull my camera out.

I arrived at the Apgar Visitors Center at 8 a.m. My tour pickup time wasn't until 8:45, so I took that time to walk a bit around the grounds surrounding the center. It was so quiet, still, and awe-inspiring that I felt a kind of reverence, not unlike being in a cathedral.

I returned to the visitor center building and headed into a restroom. A young 6- or 7-year-old girl came rushing out. "Well, good morning, Little Bitty!" I greeted her with a big smile. She smiled back and said hi. She was followed by another girl around 9 or 10 years old, who also smiled and greeted me.

"Wow," I thought, "they have to be sisters, they look so much alike."

I asked, "Are you excited for your day here?" and she replied with an enthusiastic "Yes!"

When I returned to the Red Bus stop, the two girls were intently looking at something in the bush around the bus circle. The littlest girl ran up and exclaimed, "A bird, we just saw a bird!"

At that moment, a very fit and trim man in his 40s walked up and said to the girls "Was it a bluebird?"

"I don't know, Daddy!" she replied.

I turned to the man, smiled, and remarked, "I think I've seen about one or two bluebirds in my entire life," and we started up a conversation about birds.

Next to us on a bench sat a woman with another young girl who resembled the others. She looked at me with a smile and asked, "Are you taking the 9 a.m. tour?" and I replied, "Sure am!"

She introduced herself as Anna, saying, "Well, it looks like you've already met my husband Paul." She proceeded to introduce me to the two young girls that I'd run into previously, Erin and Kimi, yet another daughter, Josie, and their teenage sons, Sean and Nolan. The kids all politely and enthusiastically shook my hand.

When the Big Red Bus pulled up and our driver, Bill, walked out, the older boys cried out, "Shotgun!" The girls argued back playfully, and the boys laughingly teased them back. It was obvious to me that these kids had been raised with much love and respect.

When we all loaded ourselves into the bus, Bill decided that since I was the only solo traveler, I would be awarded the shotgun seat. I looked at the kids and playfully gave a victory yell, "Shotgun is mine!"

"AWW!" the kids replied, with good humor.

That seat wasn't mine for long. I gave it up for an older man with a bum knee. The extra legroom would add to his comfort.

I took a seat right in front of the Adams family and had a wonderful time with them. When we arrived at the halfway point at Rising Sun, the bus stopped for lunch at a restaurant there. As I followed the group into the restaurant, I felt a pang of anxiety as I realized that I was by myself and was facing the prospect of eating lunch alone among all the groups of people. Almost as if she'd read my mind, Anna turned to me and said, "Please have lunch with all of us! Then you don't have to sit alone, and it will make our group a perfect eight!"

I sat in the midst of this big loving family and had a wonderful time. Sean showed me all the pictures he'd taken already, and the kids all challenged me to beat them at the little Cracker Barrel type peg game. Anna and Paul asked me about my journey, so I told them how it had all come about. We were shocked to discover that they lived in a town not even 20 miles from my hometown.

We also discovered a mutual love of music. I told them about my background and training in horn, and Anna gestured to two of the kids, saying, "We've got a couple of horn players right there!" The rest of the kids played musical instruments as well. Sean excitedly told me he'd recently gotten a new non-plastic oboe.

Paul asked where I was headed next, and I told him that I was headed west and would be staying that night in Libby.

Anna exclaimed, "Oh, you have to stop at Kootenai Falls and the Swinging Bridge on the way out of Libby." She explained that it was a spot of falls and rapids along the Kootenai River (the kids told me it was the spot that the movie *The River Wild* was filmed) and that it would be easy to miss if you were not looking for it. The kids all piped in about the trail, the swinging rope bridge, and how they had actually come across bear scat on one of the trails that they'd ventured off on!

"Bear poop?!" I inquired a bit fearfully.

"Yes!" they all exclaimed excitedly.

I assured them that I would stop to experience it.

When the tour was over, I left Glacier, drove three hours west, and spent the night in the teeny tiny town of Libby. I stayed at an old but very well-kept motel called the Caboose Inn.

At checkout the next morning, I stood next to an older man who was chewing the fat with the desk clerk. I hesitated at interrupting their familiar banter but waited for a lull in the conversation and greeted them with a hearty "Good morning, gentlemen! If one were driving to Spokane, what would be the prettiest route to take?"

They looked at each other and proceeded to discuss the possibilities. They both agreed on one particular route and gave me the details. The older man standing next to me said, "I've lived in Montana my whole life. I just came from that direction yesterday. When you head that way, make sure you stop at Ross Creek and see the Trail of Cedars. Be careful you don't miss the little sign; it comes up fast. Once you turn in, it's about a four-mile drive off the road, and the Trail of Cedars is about a mile long. Don't miss it!"

I had a game plan for the day: I would stop in Kootenai Falls and then stop later at the Trail of Cedars. I got in my trusty car. It was going to be another spectacular day, not a cloud in the sky and already nice and warm. After just a short drive I saw the turnoff at the side of the road with a small parking lot. I had arrived at Kootenai Falls, the largest undammed falls in the state of Montana! I grabbed my camera and started the short half-mile hike to the falls.

The falls were remarkable. The source of many of the rivers out West is glacial runoff and contains sediment from the glaciers called rock flour. When this sediment suspends in the water, it reflects and absorbs light, turning it an unbelievable shade of turquoise green. I sat in awe at the power and the beauty of the water. After wandering for a bit, I sat on a flat piece of rock and rested.

As I sat there enjoying the view, I saw a family approaching: an older man, his son, and his two grandchildren. They walked up the rocks to the very tip of the rock overlooking the falls, much farther than I had dared. I thought to myself, "That's pretty gutsy," and I pointed my camera and took a great shot. When they came back my way, I called out to the younger man, "I snapped a great picture of the four of you on the falls. If you give me your number, I'll text it to you." He gave me his number, thanked me, joined his family, and walked on.

Just downstream from Kootenai Falls was the swinging bridge. It crossed the Kootenai River, offered a great view of the falls, and connected to other hiking paths. I was determined to walk across it, even though it was high up, swingy, and unstable. When I walked up the ladder to the bridge entrance, I saw a young woman standing there, tentatively looking across at her family on the other side. I could see it was the same family I'd snapped the picture of.

I looked at her sympathetically and offered, "Kinda scary, huh?"

"Yes, and I'm kind of afraid of heights."

I laughed, admitting, "Well, we're in good company 'cause I am too. Let's walk across together. I'll be right behind you!"

We scampered across and gave each other a high five on the other side. She walked down to her family, and I heard her laugh and say, "Waiting much?" They laughed as she joined them.

I returned to my car and resumed my drive along the route suggested by the man at the Caboose Inn. Suddenly I remembered to text the picture of the family on the falls. Immediately I got a reply: "Thank you so much for thinking of taking this picture and sending it to us. It is a great picture and we will treasure it."

Smiling, I headed south on my drive. I barely saw the sign for Ross Creek on the right-hand side of the road. I turned and began a very secluded but beautiful winding drive, shrouded by unbelievably tall pine trees. It appeared completely isolated and empty. I wondered if I would be the only person there. Finally I pulled into a very small parking lot, filled with cars. I barely was able to find a spot. The Ross Creek Cedars is a grove of western red cedars, part of the Kootenai National Forest.

I started the short, mile-long trail and was amazed. I have never in my life seen such huge trees. The entire trail was enclosed by trees of such size that hardly any sunlight could come through. After walking the trail for about an hour, I made it back to the parking lot and headed west to Spokane.

As I drove west through Idaho toward the state of Washington, the past several days' events played over and over in my mind. The contrast of my behavior on my Amazing Adventure in comparison to my past was startling. In the past, when confronted with strangers or unfamiliar situations, I stayed in my safe comfort zone. I kept my head down, not looking or talking to others. I insisted that it was because "I'm shy." But I had come to realize that it wasn't true. It wasn't shyness. It was fear. I was afraid that for some reason people wouldn't like me. I had been told that often when people first meet me I appear unapproachable and intimidating. I fretted about that, wondering why in the world people have thought that.

I realized it was because my fear kept a mask on me. It prevented my true spirit from being seen and kept me from interacting with others in an authentic way. The unapproachable vibe that I put out had kept others from being comfortable with me. Because *you get what you put out to the Universe.* If you don't smile, people won't smile at you. If you put up your guard, others won't let their guard down. If you radiate distrust, others won't trust you. If you appear unapproachable, people keep their distance.

However, throughout the summer, I had made a conscious choice to look people in the eye with a smile and greet them before they greeted me. I did it at gas stations, at rest stops, at restaurants, on the trail at all the parks—every single place I went. Because of that small change that required no real effort, I got a completely different and wonderful response from the Universe and everyone in it. Because of this—truly amazing things happened:

Because I sat next to a stranger at a breakfast counter and engaged in conversation instead of burying my head in my phone avoiding contact, I had a fantastic conversation with some Montana locals and was given a generous and thoughtful gesture of some food to take along with me on my trip.

Because I smiled at little kids and greeted them with a friendly hello, they approached me enthusiastically and without fear. I met the wonderful Adams Family, who invited me wholeheartedly into their family for the day, surrounded me with love, and told me about an incredibly beautiful spot that I otherwise would have completely and obliviously driven past—Kootenai Falls.

Because I saw an opportunity to take a beautiful picture of a family against the stunning background of the Kootenai Falls—knowing that they could not capture that shot themselves and would appreciate the beauty of it—I received a heartfelt thank you in reply that made me smile and feel happy throughout the whole day.

Because I sidled up to a couple of old guys at a local hotel in a very small town as they drank their morning coffee and asked them to tell me the prettiest drive to my destination, I had a wonderful interaction with a nice old man who gave me a tip to see the grandest, most majestic-sized trees—the size of which I'd only heard stories of—and which I would have sped past without even a second glance.

Because I had chosen to follow my heart, I experienced the most authentic and loving interactions with the Universe and everyone in it. Taking a leap of faith to go outside my comfort zone was giving me reinforcment over and over that I was taking the right step.

CHAPTER 23

Roommates Reunited

A fter spending the night in Spokane, Washington, I left early the following morning and headed west towards Portland, Oregon; I had a very long drive in front of me. Because I'd heard that I must drive along the Columbia River and see the Columbia Gorge and Multnomah Falls, I was waiting to see what all the fuss was about.

Driving west along the Interstate 90 and then 395 South in Washington was fairly flat, and there was no green. It was endless fields of yellow and brown. I thought back wistfully and almost regretfully to the mountains in Montana that I'd just left behind. After a good while, I merged onto Interstate 84, and that's when I saw the Columbia River to my right.

The falls are a highlight of this little area, there are five of them, and Multnomah Falls is the most popular. I drove along a very crowded but beautiful little stretch of scenic Route 30, searching for a parking spot anywhere I could. I got incredibly lucky and pulled into a space about 25 yards from Horsetail Falls. It was breathtaking.

I'd heard that Multnomah Falls were even more spectacular, so after taking in Horsetail Falls, I returned to my car and drove along. Traffic became heavier, and eventually I saw a sign for Multnomah Falls.

It was the middle of Sunday afternoon, and the parking lots were full. I thought to myself, "I'll just see if I can find a parking spot down the road." And I'm not kidding, as soon as that thought popped into my head, I saw a tiny space just at the edge of the parking lots, perfect for my little car. I pulled in and walked back to the falls.

They were even more breathtaking than the last. I overheard several folks saying over and over how little water there was and that they were actually quite a bit more spectacular at other times. I was happy with every single view I had of them.

There were more falls along the way, but it was approaching 4:30 p.m., and the crowds were becoming overwhelming. I didn't want to struggle with that anymore, so I hopped back onto I-84 and drove the last thirty minutes to my motel near the Portland Airport.

* * *

The next day, after a quick stop for doughnuts at the famous Voodoo Doughnut shop, I spent the afternoon walking around downtown Portland, checking out the little shops and sights. Portland was unique in its preponderance of food trucks, and I enjoyed the different smells emanating from the various trucks lining the streets.

It was a beautiful afternoon, warm but breezy. I was weary from walking around, but there really weren't any benches or other places to just sit and relax downtown. I found a nice shady spot on the sidewalk under a tree, next to an awesome barbeque food truck that was cranking out some great tunes. I plopped myself down, leaned back on my hands, and enjoyed watching people walking by.

As I sat there with my legs crossed, my clothes somewhat wrinkled and my hair a bit long and disheveled, I felt some furtive glances in my direction from people walking past me. I got my phone out and posted on my Facebook page. "So, it's a beautiful breezy afternoon in Portland, but there is no place to sit. So I'm sitting on the sidewalk under a tree in the shade, next to this great food truck playing great tunes and I think by the looks I'm getting people think I'm homeless."

Almost immediately it hit me, and I replied to my own post: "Shit, I am homeless!" I laughed at my realization.

Suddenly, replies to my post came pouring in. "Nah, you'll always have a home. We'd take you in!" "You're not homeless— you're a gypsy!" "Set an empty cup down in front of you . . . the only way to be sure . . . lol!" "Play your harmonica!"

I laughed out loud at all the replies. Although miles away from any of my friends and family, I felt overcome with their love.

An hour later, I headed to the western suburb of Beaverton to visit another friend from the University of Iowa. Veronica had come to Iowa to complete her undergraduate degree after attending a few years at the University of Southern Mississippi. She was tiny, with short dark hair, a warm brown complexion and a beautiful smile. Although I'm only 5'2," I felt like a giant next to her. Veronica's native Mississippi long drawl and languid laid-back Southern attitude belied her keen and quick wit, and her harmless but sly irreverence to authority. We got along quite well, so much so that we even became roommates. Veronica and her cat Sidney moved in with me and my cat Amelia.

After graduating from Iowa, Veronica went on to attain her master's from the University of Missouri at Kansas City, and started a doctoral program at Louisiana State University before joining the Air Force service band in the San Francisco area. After leaving the service, she moved to Portland with her partner, their two daughters, and her mother. I had not seen her in the 20 years since I'd left Iowa, and I was looking forward to reconnecting with my friend.

I pulled up to her house in a very nice but hilly suburb, knocked on her door, and was greeted by her two adorable daughters, Rayna and Elia. Veronica appeared and looked just as she had twenty-some years ago.

She offered me an ice-cold beer from a nice selection in her fridge, and we settled on her covered back porch on the mild evening. I enthusiastically recounted my adventures thus far, including my enjoyable visits with our old friends Ab, Gretchen, and Pat. Suddenly I realized how quiet she was; and it appeared to me that something was on her mind. I gave her some space in the conversation.

She looked at me closely and asked, "Are you OK?"

"Yes, I'm great . . . Why?"

"You're really OK?"

"Yes, I'm really OK."

Relief washed over her face. "I was so worried that maybe you were sick or had cancer, and that's why you were taking this trip."

Chuckling, I admitted, "I guess it does seem like kind of a bucket list thing to do, huh?"

Rayna appeared, impatient to head out and show me the sights of Portland. Rayna, Veronica, and I piled into the car and headed out to get a bite to eat. After that, we ended the evening with a drive to the Pittock Mansion. On a clear day, you could see downtown Portland and Mount Hood past that. Unfortunately, it was a bit hazy, so I could just barely make out the mountain, but it was nice with lots of pretty flowers.

We returned to the house and said our goodbyes. The visit had been all too short. I felt a tinge of regret at not planning to spend more time with my old friend and her adorable little girls. Veronica's eyes welled up with tears as she hugged me tightly. I was touched by her display of emotion, recalling that she'd always been very sensitive underneath her tough exterior. I didn't ask, but I'm sure some of her tears were tears of relief that I was healthy and not embarking on a last hurrah type voyage. I hugged her back just as tightly, remembering Gretchen's statement that when there is a connection, the passage of time is irrelevant. I savored the hug, knowing that it would be a while until my next meet-up with a familiar face.

CHAPTER 24
Deep Blue Waters

While I was in Portland, so close to the coast, I remembered the Eliza Gilkyson song "Coast" and my promise to step into the Pacific. I had asked Veronica the day before, "If I wanted to put my feet into the Pacific Ocean, what would be the best spot nearby?"

She answered without hesitation, "You have got to go Cannon Beach!" It was not the direction I'd intended to head, but I had all the time in the world.

The next morning, I headed northwest on Route 26. The skies were beautiful and clear, but as I neared the coast, the clouds built and the temperature dropped significantly. For the first time on my trip I had to turn the heat on in my car. The cloudy foggy morning seemed to also dampen my mood a bit. The drive was turning out to be much longer than I expected, and my spontaneous decision to divert my route that day seemed almost ill advised. It would be very late before I got to my motel that night.

Finally, I pulled into the little town of Cannon Beach, which despite the cool weather was packed with people. However, I had no problem parking in one of the many huge lots and made my way down to the beach, where—there it was—Haystack Rock.

I had a long walk to get closer, but I did go down to the water and dip my feet into the freezing cold Pacific Ocean.

As I neared Haystack Rock, the clouds began to break, and the sun started to come out and warm up everything nicely. My spirits returned somewhat with the sunshine, and I walked down right next to Haystack and along with everyone else, observed the interesting sea life and formations in the tide pools. I was lucky enough to see several orange and purple starfish.

Satisfied with my little quick visit to the Pacific Ocean, I got back in my car and drove for a bit down 101, as I'd heard it was a very pretty drive and offered a great view of the ocean. I was not disappointed, as I snapped a couple of the most beautiful shots of the deep blue Pacific Ocean.

After a quick overnight stay in the lovely little town of Bend, the next morning I headed towards Crater Lake National Park. It was a short but scenic drive there through the Deschutes National Forest.

Once through the north entrance, I pulled off at the first chance possible for my first look. Crater Lake, formed by a collapsed volcano, was stunning. It was huge and almost 2,000 feet deep. It looked like a massive deep-blue swimming pool.

I followed Rim Drive, which surrounded Crater Lake, and drove east. I hit five of the seven highlights that were suggested in the drive around the rim. At Cloudclap Overlook, the highest point in the park, I saw a distinct line of haze above the horizon from the wildfires in California. At the Pumice Castle Overlook, I saw Hoodoo-like rock formations like what I saw at Bryce Canyon. Phantom Ship Overlook and Sun Notch highlighted a view of a tiny little island shaped like a little ship. At Vidae Falls, I enjoyed a lovely little cascading waterfall. Finally, I passed Discovery Point, where it is believed that the first Euro-American saw Crater Lake.

The highlight of my drive around Crater Lake was watching how the color of the lake seemed to change from my morning entrance throughout the day until midafternoon. As I left the park, I felt just a bit wistful and restless, but couldn't exactly put my finger on it. I was doing exactly what I'd set out to do and was grateful every day for that. I dismissed the feeling as I headed to my motel.

CHAPTER 25

A Quickie in Tahoe

T hat evening, after my visit to Crater Lake, I hit the wall. After 7.5 weeks on the road, I was exhausted—physically, emotionally, and spiritually. In the time since I'd left Kat in New Orleans, we had been struggling. Now separated by distance, our old fears and insecurities seemed to dampen the enthusiasm at rekindling our relationship, and it was tenuous.

Also, I felt a significant let down after leaving the beauty and excitement of Montana behind. My thoughts kept returning to Bozeman and Missoula, and how intimate and comforting they'd seemed, the special experiences with the people and how I'd felt like my soul came alive while I was there.

I had two more places out West circled on my map—Lake Tahoe and Yosemite—but I wasn't so sure that I had the energy to make that trek. I knew nothing about Yosemite and had no idea where to stay around there or which entrance to start from. I felt overwhelmed and just needed a break. I had booked a room that night in Klamath Falls, Oregon, and decided to add an extra night so that I could give myself the next day to find a peaceful spot, relax, and hope that my intuition would advise me what to do next.

The next morning, I found Moore Park, right on the banks of Upper Klamath Lake, and pulled into the parking lot. I took a blanket out of my car, threw it on the ground under a tree, took out my journal, and got quiet, hoping that an answer would come to me. I found myself confused and full of doubt because I just didn't know what to do next. "Keep going? Head to Boise and back to Montana and all the beauty there? Go to my mom's in Naperville? Go back to Louisville?" My thoughts swirled in my mind, and I realized I was trying too hard to figure things out. Finally, I gave it up to the Universe. I told myself to just be open, stop worrying, and trust that it would be clear to me the following day.

When I woke the next morning, I had almost fully decided to head to Boise, get through the Dakotas, and head back towards home. For some reason, though, I just did not have that gut feeling that I feel when I've made the right decision. Hoping for maybe just a little guidance that I hadn't gotten from myself, I got on Facebook and posted about my indecision:

"Good morning FB friends! I seem to have hit a bit of a wall in my trip here and for the first time I am struggling. Not sure whether to head south to Tahoe and Yosemite, or head back east towards Boise. I'm leaning towards Boise! I guess I'll decide once I get in my car in a few!"

I received an overwhelming response urging me to Tahoe/Yosemite. One of the responses, from a strong young man named Matt, whom I'd coached for about a year at DCCF, gave me a lump in my throat: "Yosemite! Why miss out on one of the most beautiful valleys in this country? Also, I'm pretty sure that if I said, "I hit a wall," in a WOD, you would help me break through it." Feeling re-energized, I headed south towards Lake Tahoe.

As the day unfolded, I started to second-guess my decision. The drive between Klamath Falls, Oregon, and South Lake Tahoe was one of the starkest, most desolate, and depressing drives I had made on my entire adventure. I certainly hoped that the payoff would be worth it. I drove through Reno and then through Carson City. I started an ascent up a mountain that was taking its toll on many cars around me. My trusty Matrix made the climb with no problem, and the landscape became stunningly beautiful.

I drove down to South Lake Tahoe, made it through the crowds, and headed for DL Bliss State Park, which I'd read offered a wonderful view of the lake. I stopped at Inspiration Point Vista for my first view of the famous lake. It was a beautiful deep blue-green color and contrasted beautifully with the green of the pine trees surrounding it.

Once I finally made it down to the lake, I was rewarded with a lovely secluded little beach. I sat up on a big rock, took my shoes off, soaked my feet in the cold clear water, and enjoyed the sights for a while. I recalled all my friends' enthusiastic endorsements of Lake Tahoe with some puzzlement. I guess I had expected something more.

The lake itself was indeed beautiful. However, the overwhelming crowds and the glitz of the hotels and casinos in town seemed more suited for couples or groups, and I felt a bit out of place by myself. Maybe it just reminded me that I was alone, and I didn't have someone special with me to share the experience with. I hoped that my upcoming visit to Yosemite would not disappoint.

CHAPTER 26
Yosemite, Courtesy of All My FB Friends

There were good and bad things about not having a schedule on my adventure. I could come and go whenever I pleased. However, when it came to getting a room on the weekend around any of the national parks in the summer, it was somewhat of a challenge, since most of the motels and campsites had been booked well in advance.

I looked to find a place to stay the night before going to Yosemite. I wanted to be near the east entrance, no small feat because there were only teeny tiny towns around there.

Actually, they were not really towns—but "census-designated areas." The closest place to stay near the east entrance was Lee Vining where there was nothing available. The next closest "census-designated area" was Bridgeport Junction, about forty minutes from the east entrance.

I got on Priceline and found a room, one of the few rooms left in town, at the Bridgeport Inn. The Priceline website indicated "double room, shared bathroom." I'd done the shared bathroom thing in New York City. I could live with it; it was so close to Yosemite, and there really wasn't another choice except to sleep in my car. Plus, it offered free WiFi, and the price wasn't exorbitant. I nabbed the room.

The Bridgeport Inn, an old historic Victorian inn, was built in 1877. I checked in and went up to my room. It was the absolute tiniest room I'd ever been in, even tinier than most New York City rooms. It really was not much larger than the bed itself.

I unloaded my belongings and took out my laptop to start blogging, but the "in room WiFi" did not work. I needed a cup of coffee anyway, so I went next door to a great little cafe and did some work. I came back to the inn and asked the desk clerk about the WiFi.

"Well, we're here in the mountains, so no surprise that it doesn't work" was the indifferent answer to my inquiry.

I replied, "I was just next door at the cafe and the WiFi there worked just fine."

A shrug of the shoulders was all I got.

I went up to my room to read a book and noticed my phone and laptop needed to be charged. I looked and looked, but to my dismay discovered that there were no electrical outlets in the room. I guess it didn't matter that the WiFi didn't work since I wouldn't be able to plug in my laptop. Exasperated by the lack of WiFi and electricity, I felt my old instinctive irritation rise up. I caught it quickly and reassured myself that this was just a minor inconvenience. I picked up Cheryl Strayed's *Wild*, walked downstairs to the large sitting room, and found a huge comfy chair close to an electrical outlet. I plugged in my phone and spent the next hour happily absorbed in the book.

The next morning, I rose early, opted not to take a shower in the communal bathroom, and got out of Dodge. I headed towards Yosemite just as the sky began to lighten in the east. It was the chilliest morning of my adventure—the outside temperature read 38 degrees. The road was deserted, and I enjoyed the solitude as I drove south past the eerie Mono Lake. I turned right and started up Tioga Pass to the entrance of Yosemite. I arrived so early there were even no rangers at the gate.

It seemed like I had the park all to myself.

I started driving farther and farther towards Yosemite Valley. I got a couple of nice shots from Olmsted Point, and then, far off in the distance, I saw a plume of smoke against the clear blue sky. I'd heard that there were fires in the area, and I'd seen smoke and haze back at Crater Lake. I came across signs that indicated this was a "controlled burn."

As I got closer to the Valley, it became hazier and smokier. Eventually I drove through the tunnel and got out of my car to see the famous tunnel view, the one you see on every single postcard with El Capitan and Bridalveil Fall rising from Yosemite Valley and Half Dome in the background. I couldn't wait.

Crestfallen, all I saw was haze as far as the eye could see, obscuring the spectacular view. Well, I knew there were still some incredible sights to see.

I was stunned at my first view of El Capitan. To look straight up at the sheer rock and know that people actually climb it—it boggled my mind.

I found the visitor center and talked to an adorable little ranger. I mentioned the smoke and haze, and she agreed, remarking, "Yes, today's the haziest it's been in weeks. But it might clear up as the day goes. I recommend you try the tunnel view later."

As she showed me a map of some spots, I noticed I'd driven right past Bridalveil Falls, so I questioned, "How could I have missed that?"

She gave me a cryptic look and explained, "Well, there's not much there." Actually, there was no water at all to be seen there. I suppose that's what happens this late in the season.

I got in my car to head for Glacier Point. The second time through the tunnel I had a much better view of the famous spot. I found a parking spot at the Sentinel Dome Trailhead. I hiked a long way to Glacier Point in the heat of the day, but what a payoff. The views were equal in vastness and majesty to those at Glacier National Park. I was almost dizzy with overwhelm looking out over Half Dome and Yosemite Valley.

I had been in such turmoil a couple of days back and almost skipped Tahoe and Yosemite to head back East, even after not really being convinced it was the right decision. If I hadn't followed that little nudge and reached out that morning to my FB friends, I would have totally missed out on that incredible visit to Yosemite. Sometimes you just have to relax and have faith that everything happens exactly as it should.

CHAPTER 27
The Good, The Bad, and The Ugly

fter my last true "out West" adventure in Yosemite, it was finally time to head back East. At the onset of my summer journey, I had left myself open to the Universe and to the idea of finding a new place to call home. I had fallen in love with Sedona, Flagstaff, and Montana although I still loved Louisville and thought that maybe a reconciliation with Kat was possible. I'd told myself throughout my trip to stay in the moment, enjoy every single thing in the present, and not dwell on the "what ifs" of the future.

But, as I turned east and approached the final month of my adventure, I found myself focusing on the end of my trip and the questions surrounding that: what would I do when it was over? Where would I decide to settle? What about my relationship with Kat, was it even possible? What would I do? Where would I live? What kind of job would I get?

The harder I tried to figure it out, the more stressed I became. And suddenly, amidst that confusion, I remembered my hike down the trail in Sedona. I realized that the more I tried to figure out the correct next step, the harder my life became. But if I just let go and went with the flow—trusted my step—the universe would open to me and the decision would become clear. In fact, I knew that the answer was already out there, and when the time was right, it would come to me. At that moment, I made a decision to let go of fear and worry, open my heart, trust my step, and let life lead me to the path that would appear.

The next few days I drove for many hours. I headed east on Interstate 80 through the gorgeous Tahoe National Forest and the famous Donner Pass in eastern California. I continued through the state of Nevada, mostly barren except for one pretty little town called Elko surrounded by the Ruby Mountains. Next I drove across Utah through the desolate Great Salt Lake Desert. I hardly saw any other cars along this blazingly hot route. I felt like I was on some uninhabited hot planet all alone. It was so remote and scary that I played my harmonica to lift my spirits.

After spending the night in Salt Lake City, I hopped back onto Interstate 80 and drove all day through the rest of Utah and much of Wyoming. I made it as far as Casper before having to stop for the night.

The Good: the next day I left Casper and started the short-ish drive to South Dakota and my next points of attraction,

Custer State Park and the Needles Highway, Crazy Horse Memorial Mountain, and Mount Rushmore. I drove all back roads from Casper to South Dakota, and it felt very lonely indeed. However, once I drove into the little town of Custer, there was no lack of people. The nearby town of Sturgis had been host to motorcyclists all summer, so they were everywhere!

I drove just a bit out of town and entered Custer State Park and the Black Hills National Forest. Custer State Park is renowned for its scenery and wildlife, mostly bison. I saw lots of pretty scenery but no bison.

After making my way through the park on the Needles Highway, named after the high granite "needles" it winds among, I headed for the Crazy Horse Memorial. This monument of the Lakota warrior Crazy Horse carved into the side of Thunderhead Mountain was simply incredible. It was still a work in progress, but stunning nonetheless. I toured the museum and then took the little bus trip to the bottom of the mountain. I was in awe of the grand scale of the sculpture.

My last stop of the day was nearby Mount Rushmore. Somehow, I seemed let down after seeing the immensity of Crazy Horse Mountain. What impressed me more than the memorial itself were the scores of rock climbers scaling up and down the sheer walls of granite.

The Bad(lands): after spending the night in Rapid City, South Dakota, I rose early the next day and left for Badlands National Park. It was a magnificent national park, comprised of about 250,000 acres of sharp buttes, pinnacles, and canyons blended with the largest area of grass prairie in the United States. I drove through the park on Badlands Loop Road, visiting several spectacular overlooks before stopping at the visitor center on the east side.

The Ugly: my friend Claudia urged me to take a little detour south of Badlands National Park to visit Wounded Knee. After a short rest at the Badlands Visitor Center, I headed out of the park and then south onto the Pine Ridge Indian Reservation. I had researched how to get there on a few travel sites and saw some reviews from several people warning others that the local Indians aggressively approached visitors in the parking lot. One even claimed that the Indians wouldn't allow them up to the monument unless they bought something.

After about an hour, I arrived in Wounded Knee. Upon arriving at the little historical marker, I was approached by no less than eight Lakota Indians, all looking to sell their crafts. Unlike the reviews I'd read, I felt no aggression from them at all. I promised them that I would look at their offerings after I'd paid my respects at the monument up the hill. As I walked across the street, I noticed some of the Indians approach a middle-aged couple getting out of their car. The couple immediately got back into their car and drove off. I realized that they, as well as probably those who had written the negative reviews, simply were scared. But these people meant no harm whatsoever. They were just looking for a way to make a living. What a shame that fear kept that couple from experiencing such an important part of our country's history.

I crossed the street and climbed the small hill to that famous monument. The sight of such a historical spot gave me goose bumps, and while viewing headstone after headstone, I was moved to tears, thinking of that ignominious massacre that late December day long ago when about 100 men and over 200 women and children were killed.

After I walked down to the bottom of the hill back to my car, I walked over to a pair of Lakota Indians, an older man and a young girl. We struck up a conversation as I looked through their beautifully-crafted homemade wares. I told them of my journey that summer, and the man advised me to keep my car well maintained. As he spoke, I noticed that most of his teeth were broken or missing altogether. Smiling, I assured him that I had regular maintenance every 5,000 miles throughout my trip. I finally decided on a lovely little dreamcatcher, a wonderful memento of the day. It was $20. I dug into my pocket, wishing I had more cash on me, beyond the $20, to give.

After that thought-provoking visit, I drove the two hours back to the interstate through the Lakota Pine Ridge Reservation. I was moved as I realized that the reservation sat on land so rich in beauty, yet was populated by those so poor. I thought of the man's missing teeth and felt gratitude for everything that I had. A little perspective goes a long way. It made for a very solemn drive across the rest of South Dakota.

CHAPTER 28

Old Friends and Bittersweet Memories

On my way back East, there was one place that I longed to visit and looked forward to with great anticipation: Iowa City. I had attended the University of Iowa for my doctoral degree, and in that span I fell in love with that great small city and made some incredible, long-lasting friendships. Most of my friends within the music program had left and started lives elsewhere, and I had visited them as I traveled around the country. However, several other friends were living there, and I couldn't wait to see them.

Jen and Dawn had lived in Iowa City for as long as I could remember. I first met them when I moved to Iowa back in 1992. They were good friends of my partner at the time, and they had lived in a cute little house in downtown Iowa City with their two dogs. They were two of the most loving, warm, and compassionate women I'd ever met. Their calm demeanors contrasted sharply with my impulsive and emotional manner, and I admired that in them.

I'd last seen them many years ago when they lived in the San Francisco area. At the time, they had a young daughter, McKinley, who was around 2; they had since adopted another girl, Bree, whom I'd never met. Jen and Dawn had always been passionate about equal rights and treatment for everyone, and several years after they'd returned to Iowa City, they were co-plaintiffs in the lawsuit that produced the unanimous Iowa Supreme Court ruling that gave same-sex couples the right to marry.

I couldn't wait to see them after all these years. I was longing for company after being alone for the past month.

I made the long drive from Sioux Falls, South Dakota, to Iowa City on a very foggy morning. After several hours, I arrived at their house, knocked on the door, and was greeted by two friendly dogs and McKinley, who at 16 was already way taller than I. Behind McKinley, I saw the wonderful smiling face of my old friend, Jen. We hugged and chatted for a bit before Dawn and Bree returned from a trip to the store.

Dawn, like Jen, was unchanged by the passage of time. Bree, a delightful, precocious 12-year-old, was smiling and full of young energy. We all had a wonderful time catching up, and I enjoyed getting to know the girls as we got ready for dinner. It was wonderful to sit down to a home-cooked meal with dear friends, fantastic kids, and friendly furry companions.

The next day, after I slept like a baby for the first time in a month, we headed out for some fun. The first stop was the Terry Trueblood Recreation Area, where we rented a paddleboat, paddleboard, and double kayak. Dawn and I manned the kayak, McKinley the paddleboard, and Bree and Jen hopped in the paddleboat. We paddled around the lovely little Sand Lake in the soft morning sunshine, talking about life and enjoying watching the girls frolic on the water.

After that adventure, we dropped Bree and Jen off at home, and Dawn, McKinley, and I drove a short way to Wilson's Orchard, where we spent a lovely hour and a half wandering among the rows of the orchard. We picked a nice variety of apples and then enjoyed a specialty of the house, a fresh baked apple turnover from the Orchard Store. I also grabbed up a bag of fresh, wonderful, squeaky cheese curds.

* * *

The next morning Jen and Dawn had to return to work, but the girls and I planned one last hurrah. After sharing my tale of disappointment at Voodoo Doughnuts in Portland, the girls eagerly took me to a local favorite within walking distance of their house, Daylight Donuts.

We had a pleasant walk up there and chose several yummy doughnuts. As I pulled out my wallet to pay for the doughnuts, Bree, with a grand sweeping gesture of her arm, told me in a very grownup voice "I got this!" My heart smiled at the generosity of this young girl. It came as no surprise to me; my friends Jen and Dawn raised two wonderful young girls. After doughnuts, the girls had school appointments, and I had to get on my way, so we said our goodbyes.

I wandered around town that afternoon and visited the demolished site of the old School of Music, which was destroyed in the flood of 2008. It was heartbreaking that the school, Hancher Auditorium, and Clapp Recital Hall were no longer there. I almost had the feeling that since the buildings were no longer there that my years there had never existed. All my memories had no tangible evidence behind them; now they existed only in my mind.

Everything was gone: my TA office where I'd first met Ab. The office of Kristin Thelander, my horn professor, where she led me in so many private lessons. The recital hall where I'd given my five doctoral recitals. The auditorium where I'd performed the Mahler Symphony and so many others.

Rationally, I knew that my memories exist in my mind only, but the fact that the structures where those memories happened didn't exist anymore made me feel somehow that I'd lost something. Tears ran down my face in the parking lot as I mourned the loss of one of the happiest places in my life.

That evening, I met up with two other beloved old friends, Laurie and Julie, at Julie's fantastic pet product store, Leash on Life. They had been my partner Sue's dearest friends, and we had spent many wonderful times together in my years in Iowa City. Later in my doctoral program, after I'd moved to Ames, Iowa, along with my partner, I returned to Iowa City every month as I progressed through my dissertation. Laurie and Julie always graciously offered to put me up on those visits. I guessed that it had been maybe ten years since I'd seen them last. Laurie, a director at the University of Iowa Hospitals and Clinics, showed me around the store while we waited for Julie to finish up for the day.

After having only a few doughnuts that morning for breakfast, I was hungry. Laurie and Julie drove us to a new restaurant in town, 30 Hop, and we enjoyed a wonderful variety of beers, yummy burgers, and fries, and great conversation. After dinner, I joined them at their beautiful home on the outskirts of Iowa City. I met their adorable basset hound, Cooper, and two cats, Simon and Manchego. We grabbed a beer and sat under the stars in their huge backyard on a perfect cool summer evening. We reminisced about old times that we'd shared so many years ago, marveled in the revelations revealed in my summer adventure, and just enjoyed a friendship that had lasted over twenty years.

CHAPTER 29
Anchor and Refuel

I was exhausted by nine weeks of traveling and wanted nothing more than to hang out with my mom for a few days with no decisions to make, so I was so grateful that she lived along the path of my summer adventure. It was a much-needed stop.

Naperville is a quick three-hour trip from Iowa City, and I made the drive following alongside a line of thunderstorms that stayed conveniently to the south of me. When I arrived at my mom's around 12:30 and walked in the back door, I scared the living daylights out of her. She told me she hadn't expected me until the following Tuesday. We shared a good laugh as she gave me the biggest, best hug.

This was not the house I'd grown up in. My mom and dad had moved into this ranch house about 10 years earlier, when my dad's health had declined to the point that the two-story home they'd been living in became too much for him. I loved our old house, where our family had lived for almost 40 years. I was very attached to it, and it was hard to think of anyplace else as really "home."

I'll never forget the day that my folks had actually moved out of the old house. All of us were there helping, my two older brothers, my younger sister, my two sisters-in-law, and my partner Patti. That morning, Patti and I had run up to Starbucks for some coffee. When we returned and I saw the moving van in front of the house, I burst into tears. Just as I was attached to the old school of music at Iowa, I was even more attached to that house. Again, I had felt that somehow leaving that house would erase all my past memories.

In time, though, I'd grown to really love the house my mom was now living in. I realized that home is where your family is, no matter where or what kind of house. And, after over two months on the road, it felt wonderful to be in the comfort of my mom's house.

My mom, like her sister, my Aunt Pat, did not have an easy childhood. My grandpa kicked Aunt Pat out at 16; my mom was kicked out of the house at 19, with only $15 to her name and nowhere to go. She never told me what happened until she got herself on her feet and found a place of her own, but she inferred that it wasn't good. Fortunately, she possessed an amazing inner strength and grit, and she made it on her own.

At that time, my mom worked for the utility company that eventually became Northern Illinois Gas Company. A few years later, when the company moved out of downtown Chicago to the suburbs, my mom moved with it, and that's where she met my dad. She told me that he sat behind her at work and used to make wise remarks about the gap the buttons would make in the back of her blouse. She said she really disliked him and his teasing at first, but I guess he eventually won her over.

As the years went on and on, though, their relationship strained. My mom battled feelings of unworthiness throughout her entire life, starting with a father who'd called her dummy instead of her name, to a husband who was emotionally unavailable with a drinking problem on top of that. She felt in some way that the reason he drank was because she wasn't good enough, so she did everything she could to try to make him happy and prove her worth to him. She kept a spotless house, cooked wonderful dinners every night, kept herself looking good and well-dressed, kept us kids clean, fed, and well-behaved. But no matter what she did, he stayed unhappy, emotionally unavailable, and continued to drink. I can't even imagine how hard it must have been for her, but I don't think she considered leaving him; divorce was not common in that generation.

After he passed away, she had an extremely rough time adjusting to self-sufficiency and taking care of everything— bills, taxes, the mortgage—all by herself. But again, her faith, tenacity, and inner strength carried her through those rough first few years. She told me every day she made a list of what she had to do, and she would put the hardest task first on the list. She said if she could do the hardest task first, everything else after that would be easy.

Now I think she's happier than she's been in her entire life. Her home is all paid off, it's just like she wants it, she lives right across the street from her church, which she attends faithfully every day, she has a core group of friends who are really wonderful, she's in great health, and she has us kids who love her fiercely. She's settled into a really comfortable life. I admire her immensely for her attitude, her strength, and her fortitude. She has never given up, at any point in her life, no matter what the circumstances. She is truly an incredible woman, an inspiration to me, and one of my best friends.

Over the course of the next three days, I had a relaxing and rejuvenating visit with my mom. Each morning, I'd wake early after a restful sleep, amble into the kitchen, and join Mama at the kitchen table with a nice steaming cup of coffee. We'd sit quietly at the little round table, looking out the kitchen window at the chipmunks, hummingbirds, squirrels, and bunnies that inhabited her immaculately groomed backyard as the morning sun streamed in and brightened the room. We spent the days walking around the Riverwalk in downtown Naperville, we watched several Cubs games together, and I relished the opportunity to cook our meals.

I shared with her all the wonderful pictures and stories that I'd gathered along my journey that summer, along with some of the difficult insights I'd had about myself regarding my struggles with worthiness, especially my inability to attempt the Angel's Landing hike at Zion. My mom sat across me, with a look of profound concern and love on her face as I cried about that day.

Mama told me, "Even as a little girl, you were harder on yourself than anyone else."

I thought back to my childhood, trying to remember how I developed that pattern so early. My parents were not harsh and demanding that we be straight-A students or be perfect or number one, just that we do our best. But, when I did do well in school, when I did make As, when I did sit first chair in the band or win an award, they would praise me for my accomplishments, of course, as any parent would. What I think I did was start to equate that praise and attention with my own sense of innate worthiness. "You're such a good student" or "You're such a talented horn player" became my value as a human being. Of course, it then made perfect sense that when I lost the ability to play my horn, it felt like losing the only thing that made me feel good about myself. Or when I tried to climb Angel's Landing but couldn't. Or anything else at all—if I couldn't do it, if I wasn't the best, I was a failure and a worthless person.

My mom did her best to comfort me by describing to me all I've done and everything I should be proud of. Even coming from my own mother, it was hard for me to believe. All she could see is what I've done right in my life whereas I could only see what I did wrong or where I've failed. Perhaps if I could practice and learn to have her life-learned perspective regarding the resilience to life's challenges as opposed to my focus on perfection and "failure," I could surely be happier as I moved forward in my life.

Saturday morning, I woke up refreshed physically and spiritually by my visit with my mom. I hugged her goodbye and headed towards Grand Rapids, Michigan. I was ready to continue the remainder of my adventure.

CHAPTER 30

My Not Really Safe House

A fter a short visit with my brother and sister-in-law in Grand Rapids, I departed to Traverse City. It was a cloudy, cool morning, with a strong chance of thunderstorms all along Lake Michigan. I was determined to have a wonderful day, no matter the weather.

I started up 31 North. My plan was to stop at as many points of access for Lake Michigan before stopping at Sleeping Bear Dunes for a visit. At my first view of Lake Michigan, I saw and heard thunderstorms looming off to the west. I enjoyed the view of the green-blue lake before getting back to the safety of my car, whereupon the skies opened up and it poured.

The picture in my head of a perfect summer day at Sleeping Bear Dunes seemed in jeopardy, but I reminded myself not to let the weather affect my positive attitude. As I drove closer to the dunes, I noticed that the skies became a bit brighter. I stopped at another lovely little spot with a historic lighthouse and a nice view of the beach.

Finally, I arrived at Sleeping Bear Dunes National Park. I planned to drive the Pierce Stocking Scenic Drive and enjoy the view of the lakeshore. I drove along the loop and came to one of the most famous spots. I walked out and saw a crowd of people at a huge steep dune with the lakeshore 450 feet below. There were warning signs all along the top. This sand dune was the granddaddy of them all.

I saw about three folks who had just finished climbing up the mammoth 450-foot dune. They were soaked with sweat, and their faces were red. They compared each other's climbing times. I overheard someone say that one of them, a young girl, had climbed up the dune in a shocking 11 minutes. I looked down the massive dune, looked at the folks at the top, took off my sandals, and threw caution to the wind.

It was a crazy climb down this dune. Actually, it was more of a slide down the sand. I had to really concentrate to keep my weight back to prevent myself from pitching forward. I could just imagine losing my balance and tumbling head over heels to the bottom. I turned myself a bit sideways and made it to the bottom in about three minutes. I enjoyed the spectacular view of Lake Michigan before looking up to begin the daunting climb back up to the top.

Because of how steep the dune was, I found it impossible to stand upright and climb. I had to lean over, almost in a crawl, and use my hands to assist pulling myself up. It was exhausting from the start, but I took my time. I took thirty steps, then rested. I repeated that all the way to the top. It took me twenty minutes. It was one of the hardest physical challenges I'd ever done. I was covered with sand, soaked with sweat, and my legs were trembling like jelly. And I was very proud to have made it.

I dusted as much sand off me as I could before I got back into the car and drove out of the park. I continued my drive north and in no time made it to the picturesque tourist town of Leland. This quaint little village is situated on a tiny slice of land between Lake Michigan and Lake Leelanau. I parked my car in the waterfront Fishtown area, wandered into a few cute little shops, and then down to the waterfront. I enjoyed the breeze as it came off the lake and walked back to my car.

The afternoon was waning, but I had one more stop to make. Many years ago, my brother Kevin had taken the family on a weekend trip around this area. We'd stayed at the Chateau Grand Traverse Inn within the Chateau Grand Traverse Winery on the peninsula in the middle of Grand Traverse Bay. It was a magnificent winery, and I wanted to go and pick up a few bottles to bring back with me. I made the easy drive up the peninsula and made it to the winery around 5 p.m.

I walked in, grateful for the air-conditioning. I perused the wine selections and narrowed my choices down to six varieties. I enjoyed a little tasting of them before making my final decision. I brought my wine up to the counter. The girl at the register greeted me with a big smile.

"Hi there! You picked some nice wines."

"Yes—I was here about eight years ago, and I was so excited to come back and pick up some more of these great wines here!"

"Well, good! What brought you back up here?"

"This spring I quit my job, sold my house, and I'm taking a three-month road trip around the country. And just seeing what the Universe has in store and where I might end up!"

The young girl really seemed intrigued by my tale. "Is there anyplace that you've found you really like?" she asked.

"Well, I really liked Sedona and Flagstaff, and especially Montana. I was there for five days and really fell in love with it."

The young girl laughed and said, "Omigosh, I lived in Missoula for seven years."

I exclaimed, "I was there for two days! I totally loved it! What's it like to live there? And how are the winters, compared to here?"

The girl lit up. "It's a really awesome town. I went to school there at the university. Really laid back, some call it a hippie town. And the winters are way better than here because of the banana belt."

"The what?!" I asked, stumped by that phrase.

"The banana belt," she explained. "It's when part of a state is warmer than all the rest of the state. Missoula is in the banana belt of Montana, and it's protected by the mountains, so it doesn't get that arctic air that the rest of the state does, but it gets all the warm air coming in from the Pacific. Winters there are milder than any here in the Grand Traverse area!"

I thanked her for our talk, she wished me luck, and I walked out of there not only with my wine, but with an excitement that I may have just found a possibility for a new place to live. Was it really a coincidence that I'd run into, of all people, someone who'd lived in the city I dreamed of?

Traverse City was only a short ten-minute drive from the winery. I arrived at my motel, which was situated right across the street from the bay, and checked in. Walking to my room, I passed a group of three women, relaxing outside their room on comfy chairs, drinking beer, laughing, and having a wonderful time. I greeted them with a jolly, "What a great start to the weekend!" before I realized it was Monday evening. They laughed and so did I. I had no idea what day of the week it was anymore.

As I walked away from the group, it hit me that their comradery made me feel lonely. "What's that all about?" I thought to myself. "I just spent the last several days with family—I should be ready to be by myself again. I prefer to be alone, right?"

When I left for college at 17, I couldn't wait to leave home and be free of the "ball and chain" of my family. After the ending of every particularly hard romantic relationship, I've vowed to myself that it would be best if I stayed alone for the rest of my life. I'd even half-jokingly told friends that I could see myself being perfectly content as a hermit. Just me, with no one else to answer to, free to do whatever I wanted whenever I wanted. But seeing those three friends outside of their hotel room just really brought to heart that I was alone and didn't have anyone to share the beautiful evening with. Wistfully I thought of my close friends in Louisville and how we'd sit around shooting the shit just like these women were. I thought back through the summer so far and realized that the most meaningful experiences hadn't been when I was alone; they had been my interactions with other people, when my heart was fully open.

The more I thought about it, the more I wondered, "Could that belief about myself being 'better off alone' really be contributing to my unhappiness that I've been experiencing?" For years, I've been told that I had a wall built up around myself. I admit that it was true. I pictured myself in an empty house, with all the doors and windows tightly closed, protected, and safe from anything that could harm me. Protected from a broken heart, protected from not feeling "good enough," protected against feeling unworthy. But there's no kind of filter that can protect me from the bad and at the same time let anything good in.

My house feels safe from the storms, but it also can't receive any sunshine or fresh air. In trying to protect myself from hurt, pain, and heartbreak, there's no way for any joy or love to enter. Perhaps that was the reason Kat and I had struggled so much. How was it possible to balance loving someone yet at the same time keep my heart closed off in order to protect myself from getting hurt? It's impossible, and the wall that I'd built didn't work anyway.

The loneliness and unhappiness I experienced as a result of closing myself off far outweighed the risk of pain. My house that I'd built to keep me safe was making me miserable. My doing, my fault, my responsibility.

Fortunately, along the path of my journey this summer I felt that I was making small changes to open up a window in my house and open up a door to my heart. And, I felt the goodness of the Universe was rewarding me.

CHAPTER 31

A Couple of Days in the D

A month or so before my summer adventure began, my friend Dana helped me set up my blog. We'd known each other for years from Derby City Crossfit, where she'd concentrated on powerlifting while I immersed myself in Crossfit.

At her house one evening, over a beautiful dinner and spectacular bourbon, Dana and her husband, Brian, shared how they had bought and were renovating a house in Detroit.

Dana encouraged me to visit them there during my Amazing Adventure.

After I left Traverse City, during a short stay in Ann Arbor with an old friend, I messaged Dana without much hope since I would be leaving Ann Arbor over the Labor Day weekend and didn't expect that she'd be up in Michigan at that time. Imagine my surprise when she said yes, absolutely. In fact, Dana was turning 40 and was having a birthday celebration that weekend in Detroit. Perfect timing!

I'd made the drive from Ann Arbor to Detroit many times in the years that I'd lived in Ann Arbor, playing in the Michigan Opera Theater orchestra.

I arrived at their house around 5:30 p.m. on Friday, just in time to assist with the final preparations for Dana's party. Earlier in the day, Dana and Brian had received news that there would be a blackout in the neighborhood, and the plumber had disconnected the water before he'd left for the weekend! It seemed like it would be a really rustic weekend. However, the power miraculously came back on and the water was turned back on too. Party prep went into full mode. The backyard was tented, there were pretty white lights strung along the tent and a little fire pit was loaded and ready to go. I met Brian's sister and her partner, and started the celebration with a nice glass of Russell's Reserve Rye. Let the party begin!

The weather was perfect outside, and Dana and Brian's friends were wonderful. One of their neighbors set up as DJ, folks danced, and we toasted Dana's new decade. I lasted until about 11pm when I collapsed into a sleepy tipsy heap in my sleeping bag.

Saturday morning, I woke to the smell of coffee and wandered into the kitchen to find it full of yawning party guests. After breakfast and party cleanup, Brian took us on a little tour of the area. It was heartbreaking to see such beautiful houses, some of which would be worth hundreds of thousands of dollars in another city, empty and abandoned.

After we returned from the tour, we headed out in caravan to the Detroit Eastern Market. I had never been to a market so huge! Produce, restaurants, food trucks, music, and more. It was incredible. We spent hours exploring, sampling, and drinking it all in.

That evening we spiffed up and drove about ten minutes down 8 Mile Road to Bakers Keyboard Lounge, the world's oldest operating jazz club. That evening, Allan Barnes and his group were the featured act. Barnes was a fantastic saxophone/flute player, and the other members of his ensemble, a trumpet, bass, guitar, piano and drums, were top-notch musicians.

I thought back to the magical weekend I'd spent in New Orleans with Kat, where I'd sat in the crook of her arm in all the little clubs while we listened to the great NOLA jazz. I just knew she'd love this too, and sitting there, among a table of really nice but very straight and attached couples, I felt like the odd man out. I longed to have her sitting next to me. I couldn't wait to tell her about this club when I left Detroit the next day.

CHAPTER 32
Honeymoon Capital of the World

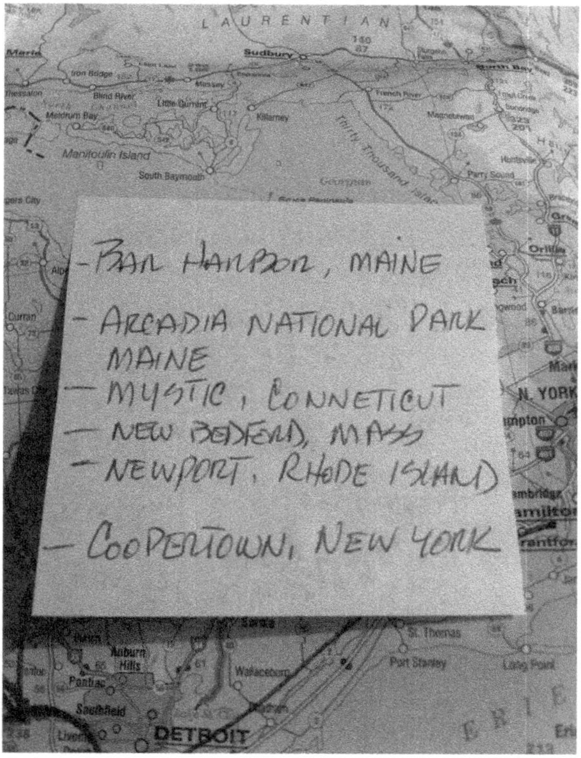
-BAR HARBOR, MAINE
- ARCADIA NATIONAL PARK MAINE
- MYSTIC, CONNETICUT
- NEW BEDFORD, MASS
- NEWPORT, RHODE ISLAND
- COOPERTOWN, NEW YORK
LAURENTIAN
Sudbury
Manitoulin Island
N. YORK
DETROIT

My original Amazing Adventure was going to end after I visited Detroit. At least that was the plan. But when I visited my mom, my brother Kevin asked, "Where are you going after you leave here?" I took out my map and gave it to him.

He looked at the map, noticing the only big blank space on it, and inquired, "What the heck? How come you're not going to anyplace in the Northeast?"

I had no reply. At least no reply that was going to satisfy him.

Kevin proceeded to write down his suggestions for the continuation of my trip. I was actually excited about it since I had been a bit wistful that my adventure was about to come to an end. I had allotted a full three months for my adventure and had plenty of time left in which to travel—now I had an excuse to keep going. As I plotted my new course based on my brother's recommendations, I noticed it took me right past Niagara Falls, so why not stop at one of the most beautiful natural wonders of the world?

After leaving Dana and Brian's, I headed east, following my brother's suggestion. It was a drizzly, dreary day, and as I looked up at the gray sky ahead of me, I was stunned to see an eagle fly over me from right to left. At that moment, my phone rang; it was Kat.

"You won't believe it, I just saw an eagle, leaving Detroit, of all places!" Excitedly I continued, telling her about my weekend in Detroit and the incredible jazz that I'd heard in the club the night before. I rattled on and on, saying how wonderful it would be if we could go to that same club together someday. I noticed Kat was subdued and asked her if anything was wrong.

"Have you decided yet if you'll stay in Louisville when you're done with your adventure?"

I hesitated, caught off-guard by the question. My stomach tightened into a knot, and I felt my defenses rise. "I don't know," I replied, feeling anxious at the question. "I haven't even finished my trip. I really didn't want to make any decisions until I returned to Louisville."

Kat paused for a moment and then said, "I think it's probably best if we just continue as friends until you decide what you want. I just don't want to get my hopes up and then have you move away."

My stomach lurched, and I felt a sting of rejection. Although I was resistant to change the dynamics of the relationship, I reluctantly agreed with her. We talked for a little bit more, and she asked where I was headed next. I told her I was going to see Niagara Falls the next day.

"Oh, you should do the boat tour," she suggested. "I did that when I was a teenager, and it was the best way to see the falls. The boat goes right next to them!"

I said that sounded like a good idea, and we ended the call. I somberly drove on in the ever-increasing rain that dampened my spirits even more. The conversation replayed over and over in my mind and sent me into a spiraling dark hole.

Our reconciliation that summer had been so wonderful, and I wanted to just enjoy the present moment. I didn't want to think about making a decision yet about where I was going to end up. I was torn—I had left on my adventure back in June unattached and open to moving someplace else. In the back of my mind I was still thinking about Flagstaff and Montana and what it might be like to move there. Getting back together with Kat had changed that, but I hadn't been thinking at all about how my decision might impact her. I wanted my decision to come to me in my own time. Finally, I realized the mood I was talking myself into and just let go, trusting that whatever was supposed to happen would be for the best.

Just then, I saw a sign for an upcoming rest stop advertising tickets for Niagara Falls tours. I pulled off and entered the huge rest stop, which teemed with tourists and numerous vendors selling tour spots. I wandered around for a bit before approaching a barrel-chested older man advertising boat tours. He gave me several options before I settled on the 4-hour boat tour. I clasped my tour reservation pass and returned to my car, somewhat lifted out of my funk.

I spent that night in Buffalo and made the short drive to Niagara Falls the next morning. The weather had cleared the night before, and there wasn't a cloud in the sky. The sun shone brightly in my eyes, and I felt almost giddy at the prospect of my day in the falls. The disappointment of the previous day came back for a moment, but I made a decision at that moment to not let it damper the day ahead of me.

After a quick breakfast at a local diner, I drove to the tour pick-up spot. At 10:35, the bus pulled up, and I, along with several other couples, stepped on. The bus was captained by a very unique guide, Chuck. Chuck was 61 years old, looked 41, with a long pony tail down his back and a cheerful face. Chuck had clearly been doing this for many years. He let us know that he was going to give us the tour of our lives, that he was watching out for us and was not about to let us get ripped off by all the tourist traps along the way. Reassured by our seasoned guide, we settled back for a great time.

Chuck was like a mother hen, directing us here and there. The first stop was the Cave of the Winds. Chuck took care of the paperwork, issued us our tickets, and ushered us into the room where we were given our water-ready, designer sandals for the day. He even gave me the insider tip to twist the straps, so the oversized sandals would fit tightly enough.

From there, he sent us down the elevators, where we traveled 175 feet below and were issued huge yellow ponchos. We got into line for the incredibly awesome deluge at the base of the American Falls.

Next, Chuck took us to Three Sisters Islands, where we got off the bus and took a little walk to all three islands for spectacular views of the rapids in the Niagara River right before Horseshoe Falls.

After a short stop for lunch, we headed for what we'd all been waiting for—the Maid of the Mist boat trip. Chuck magically found a parking place where there was none to be found. This guy knew everything. He quickly ushered us through the ticket booth to the poncho distribution point. Then, he left us in line for the boat with strict instructions to find a spot on the Canadian side of the boat on the upper deck when we boarded. He assured us this was the best spot of all. We all heeded his advice and upon boarding rushed to the spot. The boat departed, and the voyage was spectacular. We traveled as close to the roaring falls as possible. We all got thoroughly soaked by the spray, but it was wonderful!

At the end of the trip, Chuck met us and took us to the top of the observation deck for some classic falls pictures.

It was a fantastic day, and I was so grateful to Kat for recommending the tour. I have found on my adventure this summer that tours are the best way to see the national parks and attractions, and they are worth every penny.

The nicest part of the day didn't have anything to do with the beauty of the falls. One of the couples who sat right behind me on the bus tour was from Cincinnati of all places. At the end of the day, as we departed the bus, the man from Cincy turned to me and said, "It was so nice to meet you. Every time I looked at you today, you were smiling." My heart burst with happiness.

CHAPTER 33
The Gremlin on my Shoulder

The following morning, I woke up sad. And scared.

I was sad because my Amazing Adventure was about to come to an end that weekend. I was sad because I was done driving to new and exciting places. The beauty of the country and all its natural wonders was spectacular and breathtaking. There were so many places I still would love to have seen.

I was sad because I enjoyed the hours of solitude driving in the car with my thoughts to myself, with the miles of road ahead of me and the ever-changing landscape surrounding me. I drove the entire summer with no radio, preferring instead to spend the time in meditative silence or listening to inspirational CDs of Wayne Dyer and Louise Hay.

I was sad because I loved writing about my adventures, incorporating the pictures of my experiences and sharing them on my blog.

I was sad that it was over. I wanted to continue on and on because as long as I was on the road, I didn't have to face the reality of my life.

Because I was scared.

At first thought, I was scared of deciding where I wanted to live. Then scared of finding a place to live and finding a job.

But truly, I think most of all, I was scared that back in the reality of my everyday life, I would not be able to sustain the changes I'd made over this summer. I felt like I had become a completely different person. I may have looked the same, albeit with shaggier hair and a few extra pounds, but inside I felt completely different. Which was a wonderful thing. I had shed layers of unhappiness and old beliefs and habits, and felt like the true Alise. But I was scared of being different in the same environment once I returned to Louisville in that I was afraid to trust myself to maintain the new, authentic "me."

That day, I received an email from a friend I had visited the week before. She told me something that several other friends along the way during the summer had told me. She wrote, "I've always looked up to you." It was an incredible compliment, but one that I still, even after all my self-realizations, had a hard time believing and accepting—despite having discovered that I was wonderful and fun to be around and happy and strong and worthy.

I guess it was easy for me to believe in myself and love myself on the trip when I was always moving with no responsibilities or decisions to make other than where I was headed next.

But, once I returned to Louisville, in my old environment, and had to start to make some life choices, I was afraid to trust in the new "me." Because I'd spent my entire life telling myself that I couldn't, that I wasn't worthy, that I wasn't enough. Boy, those old habits and patterns are hard to break.

I'd admitted to Kat earlier in the day that I felt like I had this nasty little gremlin on my shoulder, who had reappeared and was still whispering the same old shit into my ear, and I felt like I had to find a way to throw it off my shoulder once and for all. And it was so hard because it had always, always been there.

A dear friend gave me a book right before I'd left called *I Can Do It* by Louise Hay. It was a fantastic book of life-changing affirmations, and I'd been listening to the CD at various times along my trip. It occurred to me that I should listen to it some more on my way back to the 'Ville. I was determined to find the trust and confidence in myself—and believe it and live it—for the first time in my life.

CHAPTER 34

There's No Crying in Baseball

B ecause my mom, my big brother, and I were all die-hard baseball fans, Kevin knew that I would absolutely love going to Cooperstown and the Baseball Hall of Fame. It was the next stop on my Amazing Adventure map.

I think I loved baseball from the moment I was born. In grade school, I would longingly watch the boys play pickup baseball games on the playground at recess. A couple of times, they'd actually let me, a girl, join in a game!

When I got home from school in junior high, I'd grab my glove and a tennis ball and throw the ball against the side of our brick house, playing catch with myself for hours. In high school, I wanted nothing more than to be a badass softball player. My older cousin Jennifer played softball, and I envied her strong arm and the sound of the loud pop the ball would make in the first basemen's glove when she threw the ball. Unfortunately, my talent did not equal my love and enthusiasm, and my sophomore and junior years, I played mostly as the second-string catcher on the junior varsity team.

The final game of my junior year, our team was playing for a chance to advance to the district tournament. I was excited to be playing in right field that game rather than sitting on the bench. It was the bottom of the last inning, our team was leading, the opposing team had a couple of runners on base, and we needed just one more out to seal the victory. All of a sudden, the batter hit a high fly ball, headed directly to me. It was an easy play, I barely had to move, and I put my glove up to catch it—I heard the cheers of my teammates in anticipation of the victory—and the ball hit my glove and bounced out onto the ground. As the opposing team scored the winning run, their cheers replaced ours, and I looked into the dugout and saw my coach with his face in his hands in disbelief. Words cannot even begin to describe the feeling of utter failure that enveloped me as I walked back to the dugout. No one looked at me or spoke to me, and the bus was silent as we drove back to town. I felt like a total loser. It was my fault we had lost, it was my fault that we wouldn't be advancing to the district tournament. It was the same feeling of shame that I'd experienced many years later in that Brahms piece with the Flint Symphony. Or when I was let go at University of Louisville because of my playing problems. Or when I just couldn't climb Angel's Landing. Not good enough.

The next year, my senior year, I tried out again for the softball team, and this time didn't make the team at all. I was devastated and felt like my world had come to an end. No matter how much my mom tried to comfort me as I sobbed hysterically in her arms after school that afternoon, she just couldn't dissuade me that I was a failure. Not making the team made me feel like I just wasn't good enough, not just as a softball player, but as a person. That bar of perfection I had set for myself from such a young age followed me all through my life, and anything but perfection left me feeling that I'd failed. I was starting to recognize how striving for the elusive attainment of perfection had hindered my life. I had become so terrified to fail and the subsequent feelings of shame that I'd stopped trying and settled into unhappiness. What would my life be like if I could stop judging myself so harshly? What if I could accept mistakes as natural lessons of life, instead of stamps of failure? What if I could tap into that self-reliance and self-love that my mom possessed? I was grateful that I had gradually started to recognize this and had started to take chances in my life.

I mused on my self-realization on the long drive to Cooperstown. That time of year in that part of the country, it got dark quite early. By the time I turned off Interstate 90 to the back roads that took me to my motel, it was almost pitch black.

The motel I'd booked, The Hickory Grove Motor Inn, was about five miles outside of Cooperstown, but I had no idea that meant it was in the middle of nowhere. After becoming hopelessly lost, with no cell service and on the verge of panic, I stopped at a motel (it wasn't mine!), and they pointed me in the right direction. With a great wave of relief, I finally pulled into the motel's parking lot at about 8:30 p.m. I was just in time, since the desk closed at 9 p.m. And I was luckier still when I discovered that they had discounted Hall of Fame tickets for sale at the desk.

The next morning, I awoke and looked out the back window. I hadn't been able to see in the dark the night before that the hotel was right on Otsego Lake, and I had a beautiful view of it from my window. I walked outside to take a look at the lake itself.

It was a gorgeous morning, the sun was just above the horizon, and the lake was pristine and crystal clear. I was starting to realize that summer that gazing out on the water gave me, in the words of The Eagles, a "peaceful, easy feeling." I seemed to be able to feel a connection to the power of the Universe being out in nature. I could have sat there for hours, but I had a treat ahead of me.

I made the short drive into Cooperstown and had a quick breakfast at the Cooperstown Diner. By the time I finished breakfast, it was past 9 a.m. and the museum was open for business! I was ready for a nice day of baseball education. I made it a priority to find all the Chicago Cubs displays. I chuckled to myself as it seemed that there was an excess of Yankees stuff and not near enough recognition of my beloved team. I had a wonderful time reading stories and looking at old baseball uniforms, equipment, and memorabilia.

After indulging my Cubs enthrallment, I found the women's baseball section. It was fascinating to read about and see all the women who had been part of the All-American Girls Professional Baseball League. Gosh, I would have loved to have played baseball.

Next, I went into the room celebrating baseball in the movies and saw memorabilia and movie clips from some of my favorite baseball movies of all time: *A League of Their Own*, *Field of Dreams*, and *Bull Durham*.

Satisfied with my four-hour visit, I headed out. On the way out, I passed by Otsego Lake and couldn't resist one more photo. What a lovely, peaceful place.

CHAPTER 35

Brother Knows Best

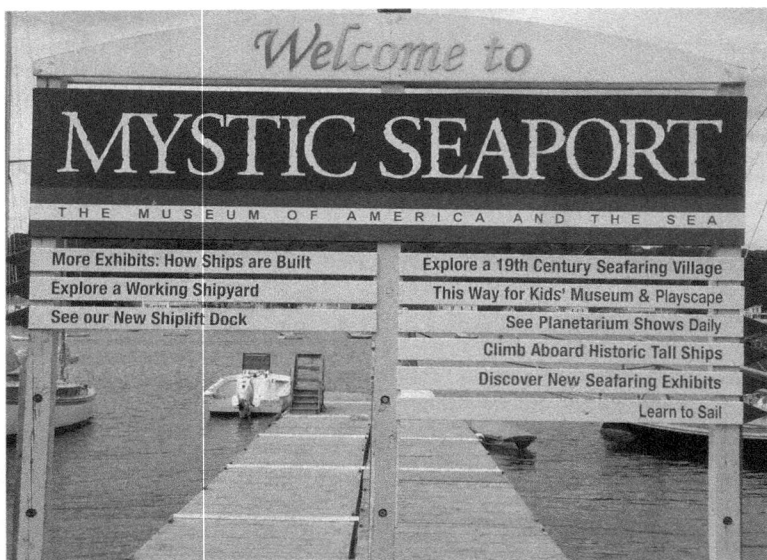

L obster rolls . . .

My brother's eyes seemed to glaze over as he talked about this delicacy that I must be sure to have while visiting the Providence, Rhode Island area. I had no idea what they were like. I pictured something off of a sushi menu. Kevin told me I would be in for a surprise.

I'd always been a bit intimidated by Kevin when I was growing up. Six years separated us, although to me it felt like much more than that. My mom told me that after I was born, my dad traveled a lot and wasn't around much. As a baby, I thought Kevin, who changed me and took me for walks in my stroller, was my dad, and I started to call him "Daddy." My mom would motion to my father, saying, "No, this is your daddy," but I couldn't make sense of that. So, instead I called him "Papa" and then eventually realized Kevin was my big brother.

Kevin took his big brother responsibility very seriously and, therefore, was more of a disciplinarian than my other more easy-going brother Joe. Perhaps that's why I was scared of him.

One Christmas, when I was very young, maybe around 8 or so, I was snooping into my presents under the tree. I was dying to get a particular toy, so I was carefully trying to untape the corner of the package I thought it was in to see for sure. Something caught my eye, and I looked up to see Kevin peeking at me around the corner of the dining room. Caught in the act, I felt ashamed and was sure he was going to tell on me, and I would be in trouble for sneaking a peek at my gift.

The summer before I started high school, I started hanging around a kind of rough crowd at Centennial Beach, where I swam every day of every summer ever since I was a kid. These kids were smokers, so, of course, to fit in I started smoking myself. I thought I was so slick. If I swam after smoking cigarettes, my parents surely wouldn't smell it on me.

One afternoon, when I thought I was home alone, I was smoking in my bedroom. I foolishly thought that if I leaned out the window as I smoked, no one in the house would be the wiser. How wrong I was. I closed up my window, thinking I'd fooled everyone. Suddenly Kevin walked in with a serious look on his face. My heart pounded with fear, and my stomach lurched.

In a stern, quiet voice, Kevin informed me, "If I EVER smell that coming from this room again, there will be hell to pay."

I never smoked another cigarette again. Ever. And my fear of him grew.

Years passed and the distance between us was ever present. We just didn't have anything in common. The age difference kept us from ever attending the same school at the same time. He was a boy, I was a girl. He was totally into cars and motorcycles, which interested me none. Then he left home and got married. I went away to college, and we seemed even further apart.

However, one Christmas many years later that all started to change. My partner Patti and I had come to my family's house for the holiday. At that time, Kevin was having a rough transition between jobs. One night, Patti stayed up until the wee hours of the morning talking to him. They had a lot in common; they were almost the same age, they both had kids, and they both had had some challenging life experiences. Kevin and Patti became friends, and in some kind of a way, she acted as a bridge between the two of us. She became the common element in my and Kevin's relationship.

From then on, I felt more relaxed with him, and he seemed more approachable. Was it just my perception of him that had changed? In any case, I felt like he interacted with me as an adult peer instead of as a little sister.

A few years later, Patti and I joined Kevin and his wife, Karen, her parents, and my younger sister Renee for a wonderful little driving tour of the Traverse City area. Kevin was relaxed and excited as he acted as our tour guide, and I felt so at ease around him.

Some years later, we had more opportunities to spend some time together. Every February, his job brought him to Louisville for a convention. He would stay with me at my house and always make time to take me to dinner during his stay. How wonderful it was for me to really get to know him as an adult. It reminded me of how scared I'd been of Aunt Pat as a child and then finding out that she wasn't scary at all!

Finally, the most gratitude I felt in my relationship with Kevin was how unconditionally supportive he'd been earlier in the year when I made the decision to take my leap of faith and embark on this adventure. I realized that he hadn't ever been intimidating or judgmental at all. He was my big brother who just wanted me to find myself and be happy.

* * *

After my lovely visit in quaint historic Cooperstown, I made the drive to the next area that Kevin had recommended I visit: Warwick, Rhode Island, just south of Providence, right on Greenwich Bay. I arrived around dinnertime, so with my tummy rumbling, I wasted no time in searching for the best lobster roll around my motel. I found a highly recommended spot, Rocky Point Clam Shack, just a half-mile from my motel. How could I go wrong with a cute little lobster atop the building?

I went up to the counter and admitted I'd never had a lobster roll. The girl told me I had a choice when it came to lobster rolls: hot with butter or cold with mayo. Kevin hadn't told me there were options when it came to lobster rolls! I thought for just a second and opted for the hot sandwich. I chose a side of fresh-looking slaw. A few minutes later, after parking myself on a picnic table with a tall can of Yuengling's, I was rewarded with a magnificent delicacy.

It was freakin' delicious. The bread was fresh and toasted. The big chunks of lobster were juicy and succulent. I pretty much demolished the whole thing in a matter of minutes. Now I knew what Kevin had been so excited about!

After a good night's sleep, I hit the road early in the day and headed southwest to the little town of Mystic, Connecticut. Kevin had suggested that I visit Mystic Seaport, the largest living maritime history museum in the world, notable for its huge collection of boats and sailing ships, and for the re-creation of an entire 19th-century seafaring village. I'd never sailed, and I'd been on very few boats in my life, but I was up to educating myself a bit.

First, I toured the large shipyard where all the renovations on the numerous ships harbored there are performed. Several craftsmen, using the original techniques and tools of shipbuilding, were busy working on several different ships at once. I was in awe to see history preserved this way.

Next, I toured the prized resident of Mystic Seaport. It's the Charles W. Morgan, the only surviving wooden sailing whaling vessel. Originally built and launched in 1841, this vessel must be continually renovated in order to be preserved. If not, the ship would gradually deteriorate and be destroyed. Visitors were allowed to walk around the ship, and it was really fascinating. That is, unless you actually had to live on it at sea among a whole crew of smelly seamen.

After three and a half hours touring Mystic, I got in the car and made the short drive to Newport to enjoy the second half of my day. I wanted to do something that would incorporate some physical activity along with the sights of Newport, specifically the beautiful homes and the lovely oceanfront. Lucky for me, I discovered the beautiful 3.5-mile Newport Cliff Walk that fit the bill perfectly. On one side of me I had a view of the shoreline and the beautiful Easton Bay. On the other, I could see the stunning, huge mansions of the area's rich and famous.

The Cliff Walk was mostly paved, but a couple of sections spanned rough rocky outcrops that I had to carefully negotiate. There are also a few sections that are precariously close to the edge of some pretty steep drop-offs; I hugged one side of the path as I passed those scary parts. It was peaceful along the way; I passed very few people but had many seabirds keeping me company as I walked in the late afternoon sunshine.

As the shadows started to lengthen, I finally made it back to my car, exhausted after a day full of new sights and sounds. Kevin certainly hadn't steered me wrong. I headed back to my motel to rest and prepare for the final spot on my Amazing Adventure map: Bar Harbor and Acadia National Park.

CHAPTER 36
A Decision in the Sand

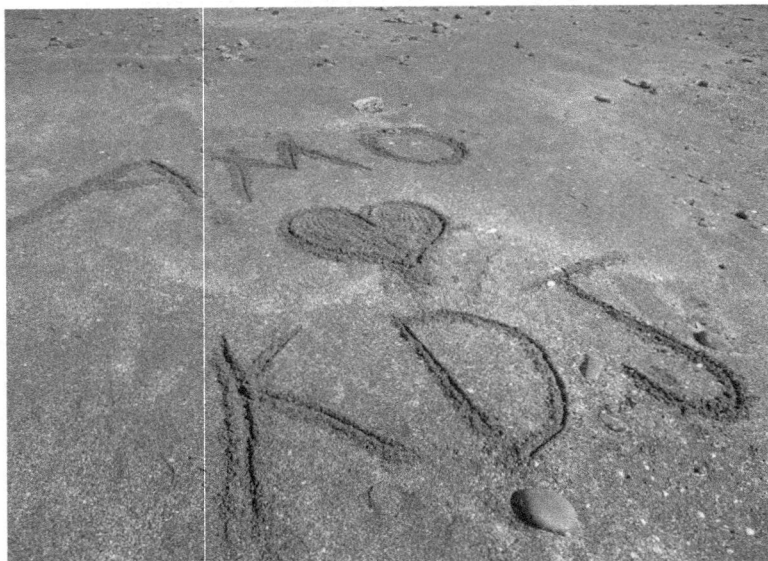

The next morning, I departed en route to the final state on my map: Maine. I hopped onto 495 and avoided the craziness of the Boston area, and once clear of that, turned onto Interstate 95 North and settled back. I passed quickly through New Hampshire and all of a sudden found myself in Maine.

I enjoyed a beautiful drive to Bangor. The interstate was lined with lush trees. The air smelled cool, a hint of the nearing autumn season. I found my motel, unpacked quickly, and then got back in my car and drove across the Penobscot River to Brewer.

I soon arrived at the Eagle's Nest restaurant, a picturesque spot directly on the banks of the Penobscot. It was so small I almost missed it! I took a seat at the rear of the restaurant to have a view of the river through the large picture window. It looked so remote that I half expected to see a moose emerge from the woods onto the banks of the river.

The waitress handed me my menu and walked away before I could say there was no need for a menu; I knew exactly what I'd be ordering. After a few minutes, she returned, and I smiled expectantly.

"What'll ya be getting'?" she inquired.

Brightly, I replied "I've been travelling around the country all summer and the past week I've been trying as many lobster rolls as I can!" As I spoke, I noticed that her stern expression never changed, and I was a bit unnerved—my enthusiasm all summer had seemingly always been met in kind.

"Ayuh," she replied in the flat Maine dialect. "We've got the finest kinda lobstah roll in the area. It's the biggest one around."

"OK, that's what I'll have." She turned and walked away, and I realized that I felt like I'd walked right into a Stephen King novel—here was the bristly Maine attitude I'd read about.

My lobster roll arrived, and it was indeed the hugest one yet. There was almost too much lobster meat piled onto the toasted hot dog bun. I completely abandoned the accompanying French fries, or else I never would have finished the sandwich. After enjoying my meal and the view a bit longer, I returned to my motel and turned in for the night.

The next morning, I woke excited to experience Bar Harbor and see Acadia National Park. I left around 7 a.m. and enjoyed the hour and a half drive along State Road 1A. Around 8:30, I arrived in Bar Harbor. I was lucky enough to find a parking place under the shade of a tree with no meter or time restriction. It was also just a block and a half walk from Bridge Street and the beach across from Bar Island.

The weather was ideal; there were a few fluffy white clouds in the deep blue sky, and a cool, refreshing breeze. I walked down to the little beach and saw several cars backing down the sand and folks unloading their kayaks and canoes. Hard to believe that at low tide later in the day there would be no water and you could walk right across to Bar Island!

After watching people paddle away for the day, I walked up to a great little pier and smelled the delicious scent of coffee and baked goods. I followed my nose and found Grumpy's Whale Watch Cafe. I noticed the window to the bakery part of it was open and on display were several beautiful pies and a platter of muffins. Oh, the smell! I went inside and picked out a magnificent blueberry muffin and a strong cup of coffee. I sat out on a picnic table, watching the boats along the pier and the increasing crowd.

The night before, I'd booked a trolley tour of Acadia National Park, so after I finished my breakfast, I walked over to a little gift shop that was the tour base. The big red trolley pulled up in the circular drive, and I boarded and settled back for the 2.5-hour tour.

There were three stops at particular points of interest on the tour. The first was the view from the summit of Cadillac Mountain. The elevation of about 1,500 feet allowed a spectacular view of all sorts of little islands in Frenchman Bay, cruise ships, and the gorgeous sky, as far as I could see. The tour guide said that Cadillac Island is the first place to view the sunrise in the United States in the fall. I could only imagine how incredible that would be.

The next stop was Thunder Hole, a small inlet, cut into the rocks, where the waves roll in. At the end of this inlet was a little cavern, and when the waves rush in, air and water were forced out, and it sounded like thunder! What a natural wonder. The last stop was Sieur de Monts Spring, which featured some lovely gardens.

The tour brought us back to the downtown area, and I got off the bus and walked back to the little beach that I'd seen that morning. To my amazement the water was gone! I wandered along the sand, across to Bar Island, joining the throngs of others for the search of lovely little shells. Seagulls and other sea birds were also taking advantage of the exposed bottom and getting a late afternoon snack.

As the afternoon waned and I meandered across the sand in the warm sunshine on the final day of my summer adventure, I took a deep breath and my whole body relaxed. A wave of emotion washed over me, and my heart felt like it had cracked wide open. Like a movie reel, I replayed the entire summer in my mind, reaching out to Kat and reconnecting, our special days together in New Orleans, and all that I had learned about myself and my fears.

Flush with emotion, I impulsively picked up a stone and in the sand drew our initials with a heart between them. As I looked down at it, I smiled, and suddenly the decision I'd been waiting for all summer long became crystal clear. I would stay in Louisville and be with Kat.

I wandered back to my car as the late afternoon shadows stretched across the sidewalk. My step was light, and I felt a sense of joy at finally making the decision about the future.

The next day, I would head back home. The Amazing Adventure had come to an end, and a new one was about to begin.

Epilogue

Prior to starting my journey, I thought it would be about creating a "new Alise" along the way. But what I discovered was that there was no need to "create" anything new at all. My true self, whom I could implicitly trust, had always been there. But, I didn't have access to her. I was unable to trust my own step because my energy was clogged with the debris of my false beliefs, insecurities, and fears. I kept that debris in place my whole adult life and buried it under a compulsion to do something every single minute of each day: working out, job, housecleaning, laundry, yardwork, VOICES, socializing with friends, Facebook. My busy-ness kept me from ever knowing my true self. It was as if distracting myself with enough activity would keep the monster of my unhappiness at bay. But all that did was act like a pressure cooker, until my unhappiness just bubbled over.

Finally, on my trip, I let go of everything and all of my distractions. I was able to relax with just myself and face my thoughts and feelings. I discovered that underneath all of the accumulated debris that my ego had convinced me was protecting me was my real, true self.

Each day, with all my courage, I uncovered and unloaded that debris of fear, hurt, anger, and unhappiness that had weighed me down. I gradually began to let it go, allowing my intuition to finally emerge and be available to me.

I am living proof that it is never too late to turn your life around and do what makes you happy—not what you think you should be doing, based on those "shoulds" of our society, teachers, family, or friends.

Take a chance, make a leap of faith, face your fears! When you imagine looking back on your life years from now, think about being able to say, "I'm so glad I was brave enough to pursue my dreams," rather than, "I wish I hadn't been so scared to try."

Trust the Universe. It will support you when you go for your dreams and your purpose. Take a leap of faith, trust the Universe, and always trust your step.

I named my journey Alise's Amazing Adventure. I realize now that my whole life has been an Amazing Adventure. And I am overwhelmingly grateful for every single thing that has happened along the way: the happiness, the joy, the victories, the hardships, the heartbreaks, the defeats. I'm grateful to the Universe for teaching me all of those lessons. I look forward to more adventures ahead, and I can honestly say that I look forward to and welcome the challenges.

Acknowledgments

Thanks to all who helped support me in the creation of this book. I am grateful for the assistance, motivation, encouragement, guidance, and advice given to me along the way.

Thanks to my friends and family who hosted me as I traveled across the country: Ab Pack, Tim and Gretchen Williams, Jody Prince, Bern Dedinsky, Pat Hughes, Dustin and Paula Werner, Tonya Moore and Chris Halstead, Jen and Dawn Barbouroske, Julie Phye and Laurie Smith, Dawn, Kevin, and Karen Oliver, Dean Hubbs, Dana and Brian McMahan, and Nancy Hubbs and Michael Heydrich. I am so grateful to all of you for opening your homes to me, feeding me, and doing my laundry! I continue to cherish every moment I spent with you. You were anchors for me as I traveled alone around the country.

To my entire family, Dawn Oliver, Kevin and Karen Oliver, Joe and Kathleen Maltese-Oliver, and Renée Oliver, thank you for your unquestioning support with my decision to undertake my Amazing Adventure.

Thank you to my dearest friend, Kat Joyner, for walking our spiritual path together.

Thank you to Patti Brendler-Hall, who encouraged me to be brave, follow my heart, and take a leap of faith.

Thank you to Erin Stimac, for being a pillar of support for me in the months leading up to my adventure. You gave me a shoulder to cry on and kicked me in the butt at the same time.

To my dear Dan Martin, thank you from the bottom of my heart for always being there when I need you.

To Nancy Pile, my extraordinary editor, my heartfelt gratitude. This version of *Trust Your Step* would never had happened without you recognizing that there was more to the original version. You had faith in me, a writer you knew virtually nothing about, to delve deep into myself and share my soul. You saw the potential and enabled me to create the book that I've dreamed of for the past three years. Thank you from the bottom of my heart.

Thanks to Debbie Lum, on our second collaboration together. There was never any question in my mind as to who would work with me on this project! I'm so grateful for your meticulous attention to detail. I can also never thank you enough for recommending Nancy to me.

About the Author

Alise Oliver is, at her soul level, a teacher. Her purpose in life is to inspire and motivate others to be the best version of themselves that they can be. She is gifted in helping people realize that they are stronger and more capable than they think they are.

Alise is an American Council of Exercise certified personal trainer. She created an immensely popular group fitness class, Cardiofit, for the YMCA Norton Commons in Louisville, Kentucky. In addition, she is a CrossFit Level 1 certified instructor and coached CrossFit classes at Derby City CrossFit in Louisville.

Alise is the author of *The Trainer's Big Book of Bootcamps: Ready-Made Workouts for Your Bootcamp or Group Fitness Class*. Alise is a certified Law of Attraction Life Coach, and she currently lives in Louisville.

To learn more about Alise Oliver, visit her at:
www.alisesamazingadventure.com.